A NATURAL HISTORY OF SCRIPTURE

A NATURAL HISTORY OF SCRIPTURE

HOW THE BIBLE EVOLVED

Keith H. Adkins

Copyright © 2010 by Keith H. Adkins
All rights reserved.

ISBN: 9781453708835

Made in the USA

A ChrisJen Publication

*Dedicated to
my wife
Yvonne,
my heart's desire;
and
my children
Christopher
and
Jennifer,
my soul's delight.*

Contents

Acknowledgments xi
List of Figures xii
Chronology xiii
Introduction xxi

Part One
Prenatal Stage: Storytellers 1

1 Oral History: The Theory of Common Descent 4

Part Two
Infant Stage: Writers 19

2 Written History: Earliest Fossils in the Bible 21
3 Prophets: First Branch of a New Species 38

Part Three
Adolescent Stage: Editors 56

4 Priests: Gradualism in Action 58
5 Translators: Diversity Strikes Again 80
6 Evangelists: Adaptation at Work 107

Part Four
Adult Stage: Standardizers 143

7 Politicians: Natural Selection in Process 145
8 Publishers: Elements of Microevolution 179

Conclusion 210
Bibliography 213
Appendices 224
Glossary 231
Scriptural Index 244
General Index 255
Endnotes 265

Acknowledgments

I wish to thank the Rev. Dave Raines, from Ebbert Memorial United Methodist Church in Eugene, Oregon for reading through an early draft of my manuscript and offering many important suggestions. His friendship and encouragement since Seminary have moved me forward in many ways over the last three decades.

Thanks also goes to my Bible Study participants from Saint James West United Methodist Church in Evansville, Indiana: Dorothy Bacon, Dick Dill, Shirley Dill, Sonie Edwards, Beverly Finn, Marshall Finn, Eva Hall, Ann Hettenbach, Mary Krack, Aleene Mackey, Bill Mackey, Meredith Maier, Sylvia Maier, Bill Mayberry, Jackie Mayberry, Darlene McDurmon, Gene McDurmon, Martha Ritter, Elsie Seifert, Phil Seifert, Earl Stein, and Ardella Wilson. Their constant support through six years of Bible Study kept my vigor renewed for teaching serious Bible Study to laity.

My heartfelt gratitude goes to Barry and Ellie Lively, Dick and Mary Davis, and Jim and Priscilla Bethel from Church of the Saviour, a United Methodist Fellowship in Indianapolis, Indiana. Their skills and kindness had a major impact on the early evolution of the manuscript. Also, I would like to offer my appreciation to Debb Ebersole of Irvington United Methodist Church for her formatting suggestions.

And finally a deep thank you to my wife, the Reverend Doctor Yvonne Cuenca Oropeza, whose support, encouragement, suggestions, and insight through the years have helped me in untold ways.

List of Figures

Figure 1:	The Northern Kings	31
Figure 2:	Genesis 1:1-2:3 and Enuma Elish	68
Figure 3:	The Septuagint	90
Figure 4:	The Pseudepigrapha	93
Figure 5:	The Dead Sea Scrolls	100
Figure 6:	The Latter Prophets	105
Figure 7:	The Q Gospel	120
Figure 8:	Jesus of History/Christ of Faith	142
Figure 9:	The Nag Hammadi Library	151
Figure 10:	The Apocrypha	159
Figure 11:	A Comparison of Old English Translations	188
Figure 12:	Ancient Manuscript Names	207
Figure 13:	Numbers of Canonical Books by Religion	210

Chronology

Before Christ (B.C.)*

3200 Cuneiform writing is invented in Sumer.
2700 The *Epic of Gilgamesh* is recorded.
2500 Papyrus is used in Egypt as writing material.

Oral History

2000 The stories of Abraham, Isaac, Jacob, and Joseph begin.
1700 The Hebrews descend to Egypt to escape famine.
1270 Moses leads the Hebrew exodus from Egypt.
1230 Joshua leads the Israelite invasion of Canaan.
1200 Israelite tribal life begins under the leadership of judges.
1020 The early monarchy begins when Saul is chosen as the first king.
1000 David is anointed as the second king, then unites the monarchy.
 961 Solomon becomes third king, then builds the first temple.

---

*I have chosen to use the popular BC/AD nomenclature rather than the more appropriate BCE (Before the Common Era)/CE (Common Era) terminology, since this book is aimed at a popular audience.

Written History

- 950 The Yahwist source begins, as the first biblical document.
- 922 The Kingdom divides to the north as Israel and to the south as Judah.
- 917 The Court Narrative begins, as the second biblical document.
- 869 Elijah then Elisha, begin their prophetic work.
- 850 The Elohist source begins, as the third biblical document.

Prophets

- 750 Amos then Hosea, begin their prophetic work.
- 742 Isaiah then Micah, begin their prophetic work.
- 722 Assyria conquers Israel and deports the ten tribes.
- 715 Judah's King Hezekiah begins reforms.
- 700 The Deuteronomic source begins, as the fourth biblical document.
- 650 The Deuteronomistic History begins, as the fifth biblical document.
- 635 Zephaniah then Jeremiah, begin their prophetic work.
- 621 Judah's King Josiah begins reforms.
- 615 Habbakuk then Nahum, begin their prophetic work.
- 590 Ezekiel begins his prophetic work.

Priests

- 586 Babylon conquers Jerusalem; the first temple is destroyed, and the remaining two tribes are exiled.
- 580 Ezekiel continues his prophetic work.
- 540 A prophet works in the name of Isaiah.
- 539 Persia conquers Babylon.
- 538 Sheshbazzar leads a first return to the promised land.
- 520 Zerubbabel leads a second return to the promised land.
- 516 The second temple is completed.
- 500 The book of Job is written.
- 490 The Priestly source begins.
- 480 The Law and the Former Prophets are edited and canonized.
- 458 Ezra leads a third return to the promised land.
- 445 Nehemiah leads a fourth return to the promised land.
- 420 The postexilic prophecies of Obadiah, Haggai, Zechariah, Joel, Malachi, and Jonah are recorded.
- 410 Six hundred years worth of poems are recorded in the book of Psalms, collected for use in temple worship.
- 400 The Chronicler's History is recorded.

Translators

- 332 The Greeks conquer Palestine.
- 300 Seven hundred years worth of wisdom sayings are collected and recorded in the book of Proverbs.

280 Five scrolls are collected for use in the Festivals: Song of Solomon, Ruth, Lamentations, Ecclesiastes, Esther.
250 The Hebrew Scriptures are translated into Greek in Alexandria and named the Septuagint.
240 The Pseudepigrapha begins.
200 The Hebrew Scriptures are translated into Aramaic in Babylon and named the Targumim.
167 The Maccabean revolt.
165 The book of Daniel is recorded.
150 The Dead Sea Scrolls begin.
100 The Latter Prophets are canonized.

Evangelists

63 Rome conquers Jerusalem.
37 Herod is named ruler.
4 Jesus is born.

Anno Domini (A.D.)

26 Pontius Pilate appointed prefect of Judea.
29 Jesus is crucified in Jerusalem.
30 Peter, James, and John begin the early church movement.
50 Paul begins writing: 1 Thessalonians, Galatians, Philemon, Philippians, 1 Corinthians, 2 Corinthians, and Romans.
55 The "Q" gospel is recorded.

- 66 The first Jewish war begins.
- 67 Qumran is destroyed.
- 70 The second temple is destroyed and the gospel of Mark is written.
- 73 The first Jewish war ends with the taking of Masada.
- 75 1 Peter is written.
- 80 Josephus begins writing *The Jewish War*, then the *Jewish Antiquities*.
- 85 James is written, followed by Colossians and Hebrews.
- 88 The gospel of Matthew is recorded.
- 90 The Writings section of the Hebrew Scriptures is canonized, followed by the closing of the Hebrew Scriptures.
- 91 The gospel of Luke and the Acts of the Apostles are written.
- 92 Jude is completed, followed by Ephesians.
- 95 The book of Revelation is completed on the island of Patmos.
- 96 2 Thessalonians is written by a disciple of Paul.
- 97 The gospel of John is completed.
- 100 A flurry of late writings appear: 1, 2, and 3 John; Titus; 1 and 2 Timothy.
- 130 2 Peter becomes the last of the writings of the Christian Sequel.
- 132 The second Jewish war begins, under the leadership of Bar Kokhba.

Politicians

- 144 Marcion tries to exclude part of the Christian Sequel.
- 150 Gnostics try to add to the Christian Sequel.
- 180 The Christian Sequel is edited.
- 200 The Mishnah is codified.
- 367 Athanasius lists for the first time the 27 books of the Christian Sequel.
- 383 Jerome begins translating the Septuagint into Latin, named the Vulgate, but excludes a group of books, named the Apocrypha.
- 451 The process of canonizing the Christian Sequel comes to a close.
- 570 Muhammad is born and the Muslim Sequel is eventually produced.
- 600 The Talmuddim are completed.
- 638 The Arabs conquer Jerusalem.
- 1009 The text of the Hebrew Scriptures is standardized by the Masoretes, known as the Masoretic Text.
- 1054 The Great Schism resulted in the creation of the Catholic churches centered around Rome in the west and the Orthodox churches centered around Constantinople in the east.
- 1095 The Crusades begin, as an attempt to free the promised land from the Muslims.
- 1453 The Turks conquer Constantinople.

Publishers

1454 The printing press is invented.
1516 Erasmus produces a Greek edition of the Christian Sequel.
1517 Martin Luther paves the way for the Protestant Reformation.
1526 William Tyndale translates the Christian Sequel into English.
1546 The Council of Trent officially pronounces the 27 books of the Christian Sequel a closed canon.
1611 King James authorizes a new translation of the whole Bible into English, from the original Hebrew and Greek.
1789 The French Revolution officially abandons the Catholic church.
1859 Charles Darwin publishes *The Origin of Species*, which sends church and synagogue searching for new ways to understand scripture.
1881 *The Greek New Testament in the Original Greek* is published, relying solely on the most ancient manuscripts discovered.
1885 Julius Wellhausen popularizes the Documentary Hypothesis.
1929 *The Hebrew Bible* is published for the first time.
1939 The Holocaust begins, causing church and synagogue to search for new ways to understand God.
1945 Ancient gnostic scriptures are discovered at Nag Hammadi.
1946 The Dead Sea Scrolls are discovered at Qumran.

1947 The State of Israel gains independence from Britain.
1952 The Revised Standard Version of the Bible is released.
1985 *The Hebrew Bible* is translated into English as the *Tanakh*.
1993 The latest attempt to standardize the Christian Sequel is published as the fourth revised edition of the *Greek New Testament*.

A Natural History of Scripture

Introduction

The greatness of the Bible becomes more manifest when studied within the framework of universal history.[1]

Megiddo is a quiet, pastoral strip of land, separated by some forty miles from the hustle and bustle of Jerusalem. My wife and I were half way through our ten day tour of Israel when our guide shared that this was to be the site of the famous biblical battle of Armageddon. As we looked out over the valley with its cloud-covered mountains and serene farming community, it hit us that a battle of any size would certainly end the world as they knew it.

In the bigger picture, Palestine was part of what was known as the Fertile Crescent. This strip of rare green land extended from the Nile Valley in Egypt to the Persian Gulf in ancient Mesopotamia, curving in a moon-like shape around the desert. That embattled part of the world was the birthplace of the words that developed into the Bible, and the stories that evolved into its canon. This book is the story about how the Bible was born and how it grew to what it is today. Because of my background in geology and theology, it is a merger of science and scripture. When reading the Bible, everyone uses some sort of interpretive lens. This book will use a natural history model to follow the development of biblical words and the evolution of canonical stories as seen through the lens of evolutionary developmental biology.

That brings us to the field of 'Evo-Devo,' or the evolution of development. Over the past two decades,

A Natural History of Scripture

embryologists and paleontologists have come to understand that evolution occurs over time through incremental changes in biological development.[2] Using insights from evolutionary biology we will follow the evolution of canonical stories brought on by incremental changes in the development of biblical words. It will chronicle the beginning and on-going evolution of the Bible by following the changing stages of biological development: from prenatal, to infant, to adolescent, and finally to adult.

Part One begins with the development of biblical storytellers, which compares to the prenatal stage of biological development. It traces ancient tribal storytellers in the womb of the Fertile Crescent. The development of storytellers caused the evolution of an oral canon of stories. Chapter 1 covers a "di-mester" set of stories that evolved during the gestational time of oral history.

In Part Two, the development of writers compares to the infant stage of biological development. Delivered from the womb of orality, the infant stage records the development of writers. This change in the development of biblical words saw the evolution of two varieties of writers: historians and prophets. The development of writers first caused the evolution of a written canon of stories then caused the evolution of a prophetic canon of stories. Chapter 2 explains the socio-historical setting and purpose of the first five writings identified in the Bible. Chapter 3 goes from the oral stage of prophecy to the written.

Recording the development of editors, Part Three compares to the adolescent stage of biological development. Chapter 4 shows how the priests edited the first three writings together, ultimately weaving a complete story from creation to

A Natural History of Scripture

exile. This story of the faith of the Hebrew people was then adopted as sacred, going a long way in guaranteeing survival of the evolving canon. Chapter 5 considers the natural consequence of variation, which produced the Greek-language Septuagint in Egypt and the Aramaic-language Targumim in Babylon. This happened en route to the canonization of the prophetic writings prior to the fall of Palestine to the Romans. Chapter 6 introduces adaptation, the localized result of a changing environment. Massive unrest at the time of Jesus was bound to create an adaptation of Law. The creative force of evolution was ready to produce change, and the resulting story was Gospel. Perhaps as a reaction to the Christian documents, the Writings part of the Hebrew Bible was canonized and the Hebrew canon was closed.

The first three stages of this book show the evolution of the canon of the Bible through developmental changes in its words. Part Four, the adult stage, considers the evolutionary processes occurring above (macroevolution) and below (microevolution) the story level. While Politicians worked to standardize the big picture of the biblical canon, publishers attempted to standardize the variations within the text. Chapter 7 shows how politicians became the agents of selection that led to the canonization of the Christian sequel. Chapter 8 explains how publishers continue to pursue a standardization of the text.

The idea for this book came from a series of lectures I gave on the formation of the biblical canon. When the series was over, something kept troubling me. I had just finished describing the creation of the Bible by many authors and editors over a long period of time, but the finality of the story didn't feel right. Finally it hit me. The Bible was not created in

A Natural History of Scripture

the sense that it is a done deal. It has evolved to what it is today, and it is still developing changes in the words as new archaeological and textual critical discoveries are made. Viewing the Bible through the lens of evolutionary biology is meant to give a new perspective on what the Bible is, which is basic to understanding the Bible.

As a pastor for twenty-seven years, I have found many people disillusioned and confused by poorly explained biblical criticism and media-hyped archaeological discoveries. I intend to present a different view of the Bible, a divinely inspired yet very human product, to hopefully foster a new or renewed love for our amazing Bible. As Harold Bloom says "read deeply, not to believe, not to accept, not to contradict, but to learn to share in that one nature that writes and reads."[3] The graphic at the beginning of each of the four parts and eight chapters is the natural history model, highlighting the topic at hand. The top line is about the development of biblical words, and the bottom line is about the corresponding evolution of canonical stories.

A Natural History of Scripture

Part One
Prenatal Stage: Storytellers

Prenatal Stage: Storytellers	Infant Stage: Writers		Adolescent Stage: Editors			Adult Stage: Standardizers	
Oral History	Written History	Pro-phets	Priests	Trans-lators	Evan-gelists	Politi-cians	Pub-lishers

2000 BC　　950 BC　　750 BC　586 BC　332 BC　　63 BC　　AD 144　AD 1454　NOW

The greatest of storytellers have been those who depict it.[4]

Since the dawn of humanity, people have asked basic questions like "Who am I?" and "Why am I here?" About four thousand years ago, the Hebrew people started having their own answers: "We are God's people" and "God has given us land." But that doesn't even begin to tell the triumph of their stories, because in a world full of gods, this unique group of people first had to introduce the idea of monotheism.[5] Sitting around the campfire, these ancient tribal families told and listened to words about the one God who chose to have a relationship with them. These words formed stories that were passed on from one generation to the

A Natural History of Scripture

next, and their authority came from the community, not the storytellers.

The words developed over a period of about a thousand years, gradually evolving into two distinct collections of oral history. Since development is a biological issue, I refer to these two collections as di-mesters, following the tri-mester model of human pregnancy. But did the stories preserve the full account of God's interactions with the Hebrews? The theory of evolution would suggest a negative answer. Here's why. A primary theme of Darwinian evolution is the overproduction of offspring. Because this book garners insights from biological evolution, we may assume that far more words were produced than survived. The storytellers themselves acted as agents of selection to preserve representative stories, but a thousand years is a long time to properly preserve memories. We have a hard time keeping short stories straight for a short time.

Many of us remember where we were when we got the news that President Kennedy had been shot. Try to recall the details, and things either get fuzzy or we disagree. Others remember the explosion of the space shuttle Challenger; but good luck trying to remember the crew, the day of the week, or even the year. All of us remember the events of September 11, but we have different perspectives based on our own experience. This is a good way to begin to appreciate the Hebrew Bible's Prenatal Stage, which provided the oral stories used by the first writers.

The lengthy stories surely found a variety of additions and subtractions over a millennium of storytelling, all of which affected the details. In fact, there are even now hundreds of thousands of variant readings among the existing copies of

A Natural History of Scripture

scripture, none of which are the original manuscripts. The Bible we have today is sacred for sure, but it was developed by many different people and evolved over a long period of time. The Bible is sacred because its purpose is to share about our relationship with God, as opposed to sharing about history or theology, but the words and means of transmission were very human. The Prenatal Stage was about the words that the storytellers told, and Chapter 1 starts with that very human enterprise.

A Natural History of Scripture

Chapter 1
Oral History: The Theory of Common Descent

Prenatal Stage: Storytellers	Infant Stage: Writers		Adolescent Stage: Editors			Adult Stage: Standardizers	
Oral History	Written History	Pro-phets	Priests	Trans-lators	Evan-gelists	Politi-cians	Pub-lishers

2000 BC　　950 BC　　750 BC　586 BC　332 BC　　63 BC　　AD 144　AD 1454　NOW

There is grandeur in this view of life, with its several powers, having been originally breathed by the Creator into a few forms or into one; and that...from so simple a beginning endless forms most beautiful and most wonderful have been, and are being evolved.[6]

Darwin changed everything. His dramatic conclusion that all life on earth probably evolved from a single origin became known as the theory of common descent. This teaches us to look for an originating story from which the grandeur of the Bible descended, and that simple beginning can be found in Genesis 12:1-4.[7] I call this bibliogenesis. That story begins Israel's ancestral narratives,

A Natural History of Scripture

which roots the prehistory of Israel in covenant. The Hebrew patriarchs of Abraham, Isaac, and Jacob may never have existed as individuals, but they certainly represent the beginning coalescence of a people of God. Scholars were intrigued when clay tablets in Mesopotamia were unearthed bearing Abraham's name. The problem was that many tablets were discovered over the next few years from many different centuries and cultures bearing Abraham's name. When the dust settled, they realized that Abraham was simply a popular name, and they had no assurance that the tablets were enshrining the Hebrew patriarch. For that matter, none of the patriarchs are mentioned with certainty in any text outside the Bible.

The next section will share a brief synopsis of the strands of oral stories that were ultimately woven into the books of Genesis, Exodus, and Numbers. The first di-mester of stories cover the travels of the Hebrew people through Egypt, their incredible experience in the exodus, and their subsequent wanderings in the wilderness as they seek access to their divinely promised land. Along the way they become God's people, legitimizing the story that God created the nation of Israel. Keep in mind that the following text references represent a much later stage in biblical evolution. As for now, just pay attention to the bare bones story line.

The First Di-mester

No e-mail arrived, no voice mail was left, and no cell phone rang, yet God somehow called Abram to leave his country and go to "the land that I will show you" (Genesis 12:1). "So Abram

A Natural History of Scripture

went, as the LORD had told him" (Genesis 12:4) and he arrived in the land of Canaan, where the LORD said "To your offspring I will give this land" (Genesis 12:7). Now this was a strange promise to make, because Abram was old and his wife Sarai was barren. Almost as a portent of future troubles, and certainly as a symbol of Sarai's barrenness, there was a famine in the land. So Abram went down to the Nile-enriched land of Egypt, then came back up to Canaan. Abram now began to despair of his continuing childlessness, but God reiterated the promise of offspring. After changing Abram and Sarai's names, God came through with his[8] promise and the child was named Isaac (Genesis 21:1-3).

Isaac had a rather precarious start. One day God told Abraham to offer his only son as a burnt offering. As Abraham prepared to obey, God repented. Later, Isaac married Rebekah and they waited twenty years to have a child (Genesis 25:20, 26). Actually they had two, because Rebekah had twins. Jacob was the younger twin, but he stole his brother's birthright, received his father's blessing, and had a famous dream about a ladder (Genesis 28:10-19).

Just as God changed Abram's name to Abraham, God also changed Jacob's name to Israel (Genesis 32:28). Israel had twelve sons, but he "loved Joseph more than any other of his children" (Genesis 37:3). Sibling rivalry developed and the brothers ended up selling Joseph to slave traders, who eventually sold him in Egypt. After Joseph interpreted the Egyptian Pharaoh's dream as a coming famine, Pharaoh appointed him as Egypt's second-in-command.

A famine indeed came and it spread into Canaan, but Egypt was prepared because of Joseph. Israel sent his sons to Egypt to purchase some surplus food and Joseph recognized them upon arrival. After some tests, he found that they had undergone moral transformation and all became reconciled.

Things turned bad in Egypt after the death of Joseph, and a new king saw the growing number of Israelites as a security threat. Pharaoh set taskmasters over the Israelites to oppress them with forced labor, but their numbers grew. He then instructed the two chief midwives to kill all newborn males. They did not do it, so Pharaoh commanded all of his people to throw newborn males into the Nile (Exodus 1:22). One particular male infant was hidden in a basket and placed among the reeds by the river. The daughter of Pharaoh found him and named him Moses (Exodus 2:10), which means "drawn from the water."

Moses

Moses realized the cruelty inflicted upon his people when he saw an Egyptian beating a fellow Hebrew, so Moses killed the Egyptian. When Pharaoh found out, he ordered the execution of Moses, but Moses fled. He settled in the land of Midian and married the local priest's daughter. Meanwhile, God heard the cries of the enslaved Israelites and took notice. From a burning bush, God called Moses to liberate the Hebrew people, and Moses was reluctant. Assuming a polytheistic environment, Moses wanted to know the name of this particular God, to which God responded "I Am Who I Am" (Exodus 3:14), or YHWH in Hebrew.

Moses returned to Egypt and told Pharaoh that the LORD said "Let my people go" (Exodus 5:1). After several

A Natural History of Scripture

failures to accomplish the divinely appointed mission, God sent ten plagues. Pharaoh finally relented and the Israelites departed Egypt. Pharaoh, having a change of heart, led six hundred chariots in pursuit of the slaves (Exodus 14:5). Trapped at the Red Sea, Moses followed the LORD's instructions and the sea divided. Making it safely to the other side, the sea closed and Pharaoh and all his troops drowned.

After wandering in the wilderness for a short while, the Israelites got thirsty, hungry, and angry, so God provided bread from heaven (Exodus 16:4). After nearly two months in the wilderness, the wanderers came to Mount Sinai and God gave them the Ten Commandments (Exodus 20:1-17). God then instructed Moses to tell the Israelites to "make me a sanctuary, so that I may dwell among them" (Exodus 25:8).

Toward the end of their lengthy sojourn in the wilderness, God informed Moses that he would be allowed to see the promised land[9] but not enter it. The LORD then designated Joshua to succeed Moses (Numbers 27:18-19) and warned him to have the Israelites drive out all the inhabitants of Canaan when they take possession of it. *This is the basic storyline at the heart of the Hebrew Bible*, which ultimately became the Torah, the first and most important five books of the Hebrew Scriptures. The stories cover nearly eight hundred years of history.

The next series of oral stories provides the background for what later became the books of Joshua, Judges, Samuel, and Kings. (The designation of 1 and 2 Samuel, 1 and 2 Kings, and 1 and 2 Chronicles resulted from later translations of the Bible.) These books are now known as the Deuteronomistic History, but we will get into that later. *The transition from being Hebrews to being Israelites had*

A Natural History of Scripture

everything to do with becoming a nation of God's people living on their God-promised land. The first set of stories taught us that the Hebrews were God's people. This next set of stories will teach us that the Israelites were settling on land promised to them by God.

The Second Di-mester

After Moses died, the LORD told Joshua and the Israelites to cross the Jordan. Led by the priests carrying the ark of the covenant, another miraculous water crossing was accomplished (Joshua 3:15-16). A different crossing though: the crossing of the Red Sea had the enemy behind them, trying to keep them from becoming a nation, while the crossing of the river Jordan had the enemy ahead of them, trying to keep them from possessing the land. They were already a unique people from a covenant relationship with the one God, but crossing the Jordan made them complete with the gift of land. *This was the birth of the Israelites.* The lateness of the recording of the second oral library as compared to the original time of the stories, is witnessed in several references like "a great heap of stones, *which stands there to this day*" (Joshua 8:29—author's italics).

The fall of Canaan took place over a period of time, and going against God's warning, the Israelites allowed many residents to continue practicing idolatry. The Bible tells us that the Israelites destroyed the city of Jericho, and then gradually fought many wars. The gift of land was not fully appreciated until many years later when King David took the city of Jerusalem. The land of Canaan was slowly "divided among

A Natural History of Scripture

the Israelite tribes, with one exception: The members of the tribe of Levi received no territory. Instead, they were designated as the spiritual teachers and leaders of the other tribes, and were to be supported by a ten percent tax imposed on the other Israelites."[10]

This was an unsettled time in the life of Israel. The great leadership of Moses and Joshua was in the past and the great leadership of King David was in the future. After Joshua died, a whole generation grew up not knowing the LORD. We are told that

> the Israelites did what was evil in the sight of the LORD and worshipped the Baals; and they abandoned the LORD, the God of their ancestors, who had brought them out of the land of Egypt; they followed other gods, from among the gods of the peoples who were all around them, and bowed down to them; and they provoked the LORD to anger. (Judges 2:11-12)

The LORD responded by lifting up judges to bring about a measure of control and a return to God's ways. Judges were also leaders and prophets among their tribal units. Deborah was one of the judges who enjoyed success in war. At that time, "a woman who delivered a war oracle or killed an enemy general, by whatever means, was celebrated, but not particularly because of her sex; she was simply a hero."[11]

The fifteenth and final judge was Samson, who was remembered for having all brawn and no brains. Things were deteriorating in the promised land and anarchy was developing because "all the people did what was right in their own eyes" (Judges 21:25). It was time for God to act again, so God raised up prophets. Prophecy was slow to take hold, but it was finally established with the rise of the prophet Samuel.

Samuel

The prophet Samuel appeared in the Bible in various ways: a seer, a priest, a prophet, and a judge. As these roles "converged in him, so the hopes for a new day of unity and identity centered in him. What Moses had been to the exodus and Joshua to conquest, Samuel was to become for the monarchy."[12] When Samuel grew older, the Israelites rebelled because they wanted a king to govern them. Samuel tried to reason with them, but "the people refused to listen to the voice of Samuel; they said, 'No! But we are determined to have a king over us'" (1 Samuel 8:19).

Samuel then summoned all the tribes of Israel and chose Saul by lot to be their king. Since Saul was taller than any of them, Samuel said "'Do you see the one whom the LORD has chosen? There is no one like him among all the people.' And all the people shouted, 'Long live the king!'" (1 Samuel 10:24).

The United Monarchy

We move now to the time of the united monarchy, where Jerusalem takes a prominent position. The transition from anarchy under judges to loyalty under kings was an

A Natural History of Scripture

extraordinary event, but the very existence of the kings of the united monarchy has been called into question. This is because "for all their reported wealth and power, neither David nor Solomon is mentioned in a single known Egyptian or Mesopotamian text."[13] However, in the summer of 1993 an artifact was discovered that mentioned the House of David, which meant that it was "known throughout the region; this clearly validates the biblical description of a figure named David becoming the founder of the dynasty of Judahite kings in Jerusalem."[14]

The time for the birth of the monarchy is difficult to determine, because the number of years King Saul reigned has been damaged in the Hebrew text (1 Samuel 13:1) and the number is unknown.[15] The following stories provide the final oral background as we prepare for the evolution of the first written work of the Bible.

King Saul

The transition from tribal kinship to national kingship is very complex and involves social, political, economic and religious issues. However the united monarchy got started, the biblical story tells us that things didn't go very well for the first ruler. In one war with the Philistines, King Saul was outnumbered, disobeyed God, and in general had a pretty bad day. Samuel told him that "the LORD has sought out a man after his own heart; and the LORD has appointed him to be ruler over his people, because you have not kept what the LORD commanded you" (1 Samuel 13:14). Thereafter, Saul

A Natural History of Scripture

began to suffer from mental illness, which would get soothed by a young lyre player named David.

Meanwhile, the Philistine war raged on and David volunteered to fight Goliath to save his country. Killing Goliath (1 Samuel 17:48-51), David was catapulted into instant fame, or at least this is the way the teller of that particular story wants us to believe. Another story tells us that Elhanan killed Goliath (2 Samuel 21:19). Anyway, King Saul became jealous and tried many times to kill David. At one point David spared Saul's life and Saul was so stunned by this act of kindness to an enemy he proclaimed "now I know that you shall surely be king" (1 Samuel 24:20).

Troubles with the Philistines were growing, so one night Saul consulted the medium of Endor. She conjured up the spirit of the now-deceased Samuel, who informed Saul that "tomorrow you and your sons shall be with me" (1 Samuel 28:19). The next day the Philistines caught up with Saul and his sons and they killed three of his sons. Saul was badly wounded, so he asked his armor-bearer to kill him. Filled with terror, the armor-bearer was unwilling to help, so "Saul took his own sword and fell upon it" (1 Samuel 31:4).

King David

David was a favorite son of the tribe of Judah, so when Saul died "the people of Judah came, and there they anointed David king over the house of Judah" (2 Samuel 2:4). Likewise, the sole surviving son of Saul was made king over Israel and the other tribes (2 Samuel 2:8-9). After seven and a half years of civil war, "all the elders of Israel came to the king at Hebron;

A Natural History of Scripture

and King David made a covenant with them at Hebron before the LORD, and they anointed David King over Israel" (2 Samuel 5:3).

The first thing David did was to capture Jerusalem, the lone holdout of the Canaanites, and turn it into the capital of the united monarchy. For the first time in history, the promised land was being fully governed by the nation of Israel. Next he brought the ark of the covenant to Jerusalem, to solidify a political, military, and religious function for Jerusalem. Then he coveted Bathsheba, impregnated her, had her husband murdered, and married her. The LORD responded by sending the prophet Nathan to David to tell him a story about a poor man wronged by a rich man. Assuming this was a local crime, David demanded to know who it was, because he deserved death. Nathan responded by saying, "You are the man!" (2 Samuel 11:27).

David confessed his sin and received absolution, but Nathan informed him that the child he was having with Bathsheba would die. When the child was born it became very ill, and David fasted and prayed, to no avail. Seven days later the baby was dead. This began a series of troubling stories. David's firstborn son Amnon raped his half sister Tamar and was killed by his younger brother Absalom.

Even though he was next in line to the throne, Absalom revolted against his father and ended up dying. As King David aged and became feeble, his eldest living son, Adonijah, declared himself king. King David then abdicated his throne to Solomon, his youngest son. After King David's death, Solomon feared a revolt from his older brother and declared "as the LORD lives, who has established me and placed me on the throne of my father David, and who has made me a house as he promised, today Adonijah shall be put to death" (1 Kings 2:24).

King Solomon

Soon after Solomon was king, God came to him in a dream and offered him anything he wanted. After a short explanation, Solomon said "Give your servant therefore an understanding mind to govern your people, able to discern between good and evil; for who can govern this your great people?" (1 Kings 3:9). King Solomon used his wisdom well and his reputation spread throughout the land and beyond. Of course, his greatest achievement was the building of the temple to house the ark of the covenant, which held the two stone tablets of the Ten Commandments.

Solomon's downfall came with his marriage to idol-worshippers, because they brought their idol worship into Israel. Solomon's great love for his wives caused him to accommodate their religion by building temples for their gods. In his old age, King Solomon's "heart was not true to the LORD his God, as was the heart of his father David. For Solomon followed Astarte the goddess of the Sidonians, and Milcom the abomination of the Amonites" (1 Kings 11:4-5).

The First Temple

Although David brought the ark to Jerusalem and centered the religious, political, and military power there, he still needed

A Natural History of Scripture

God's affirmation of the monarchy. The appropriate sign was a temple, and it became Solomon's duty to actually build the temple, because God had forbidden David from doing the work (1 Kings 8:18-19). Unfortunately, none of the first temple has survived. All we know about it comes from the Bible and most of that information is found in 1 Kings 5-7.

The layout of Solomon's temple was simple: an entryway, a hallway, and an inner sanctuary that held the two stone tablets of the Ten Commandments (which disappeared when the Babylonians later destroyed the temple). Surprisingly the temple held no artifacts of the exodus other than the ark of the covenant. However, the mementos it did hold showed tremendous influence from polytheism. Two gigantic pillars stood at the entrance to the temple, just as one would find at any sacred site in that part of the world. Also, an altar of sacrifice was located in a courtyard just outside the temple. It consisted of a huge basin representing the primal sea, supported by twelve oxen that were common symbols of fertility and power.

Even though the temple was replete with pagan imagery, to them it represented home. Their religion was complete; they were a people of covenant in a land of promise and their wanderings were over. This second di-mester of oral stories developed over about two hundred years, bringing the events much closer to the time they were written down than the first collection. This gives them less time to be affected by the foibles of human transmission.

The preceding synopsis of the di-mesters must be understood as a collection of stories, because there was no Bible. The oral stories developed in the womb of the Fertile Crescent, but the text had not yet been born. We will now

A Natural History of Scripture

begin to look at the text, as the Prenatal Stage of biblical development had put in its gestational time.

*As this stage
comes to a close,
there were many reasons
to write down the stories,
but let's first take a look at
Guided Exercise #1
on the next page.*

A Natural History of Scripture

Guided Exercise #1

Just as Darwin concluded that a single genus of South American mockingbirds gave rise to different species on the Galapagos, the single genre of biblical oral stories developed into a variety of styles.

1. <u>Narrative</u>. Like childhood stories or exciting vacations, the power of personal experience is what makes this style of story memorable. Have someone read Genesis 12:1-8 and 1 Samuel 16:1-13 to you and see if you can retell them.
2. <u>Law</u>. Freedom is a great motivator. Knowing the demands of the community can empower a person to stay out of trouble. Read Exodus 21:12-14 and Deuteronomy 22:22-29 for examples of Hebrew local laws.
3. <u>Prophecy</u>. This is about the power of vision, which is uniquely difficult to forget. See what images come to mind when you read Isaiah 40:1-11 and Zechariah 3:1-5.
4. <u>Poetry</u>. Feelings help drive the memorization power behind this style of story. Read Exodus 15:21 and Judges 5 to capture the feelings of these ancient poems.
5. <u>Wisdom</u>. The power of knowledge has long been valued. My mother-in-law's favorite advice was "If you stand behind a donkey a second time, no one will know which one was the donkey." To taste the flavor of biblical wisdom, read Ecclesiastes 7:1-12 and Job 38:1-15.

A Natural History of Scripture

Part Two
Infant Stage: Writers

Prenatal Stage:	Infant Stage:		Adolescent Stage:			Adult Stage:	
Storytellers	Writers		Editors			Standardizers	
Oral History	Written History	Pro- phets	Priests	Trans- lators	Evan- gelists	Politi- cians	Pub- lishers
2000 BC	950 BC	750 BC	586 BC	332 BC	63 BC	AD 144	AD 1454 NOW

Writing only started when an organized system of signs or symbols was created that could be used to clearly record and fix all that the writer was thinking, feeling, and capable of expressing.[16]

Writing was invented by a group of people known as Sumerians. Located in the eastern tip of the Fertile Crescent near the Tigris and Euphrates Rivers, Sumer became the world's first civilization. Nomads gave up their wandering lifestyle and became phenomenally creative. Settling in this land between the rivers, they gradually invented the plow, the wheel, and an agricultural society. Why here, rather than Egypt, located at the western tip of the Fertile Crescent in the rich Nile Delta? Jared Diamond has

A Natural History of Scripture

forcefully argued that "History followed different courses for different peoples because of differences among people's environments, not because of biological differences among peoples themselves."[17]

Meanwhile, as Sumer grew, human memory proved insufficient to care for the various transactions needed. Born of necessity, enduring images were invented by pressing symbols into moist clay tablets and letting them harden. That is where writing began, and the Infant Stage of biblical development began when the Hebrew people developed their own alphabet. Delivered from the womb of orality, the Infant Stage records the development of biblical writers. This change in the development of biblical words, from oral to written, saw the evolution of two varieties of writers: historians and prophets. Variation is the second undeniable fact of natural selection, where Darwin theorized that each new organism bore distinguishing features. This idea was the same one that began to unlock the mystery of biblical formation, because individual historians were identifiable by their unique styles.

A Natural History of Scripture

Chapter 2
Written History: Earliest Fossils in the Bible

Prenatal Stage: Storytellers	Infant Stage: Writers		Adolescent Stage: Editors			Adult Stage: Standardizers	
Oral History	**Written History**	Pro-phets	Priests	Trans-lators	Evan-gelists	Politi-cians	Pub-lishers
2000 BC	950 BC	750 BC	586 BC	332 BC	63 BC	AD 144	AD 1454 NOW

There is no original copy of any of the books of the Bible.[18]

After a thousand years of passing the sacred stories from generation to generation by word of mouth, the Hebrew people began speaking their own language, but they had not yet invented a written Hebrew alphabet. The necessary motivation arose when God gave Moses the law at Mount Sinai. The second of the Ten Commandments said, "You shall not make for yourself a graven image" (Exodus 20:4, Revised Standard Version). Since they had been using the image-based system of their Sumerian ancestors, the Hebrew people were compelled to create a new, non-pictographic writing system to avoid making engraved images. Hebrew writing developed sometime after the giving of

A Natural History of Scripture

the law, but it took until the time of King David before it was of practical use.

The Yahwist Source

Now that their homeland was established, it was time to write down the story of the birth of Israel. An individual or group of people who preferred to use the divine name *Yahweh*,[19] wrote a story which is now referred to as the Yahwist source. The Yahwists worked from the early collection of oral stories and presented them in their own way. To introduce their story of the beginnings of the people of Israel through Abraham, the Yahwists offered a story of the beginnings of Abraham through *adam*, the Hebrew word for human being. There was no literal man named Adam, but the story was packed full of theological truth. The following is an accounting of how the Yahwists developed their biblical account of creation and how the historical setting affected the story.

Creation

The Yahwist creation story (Genesis 2:4-25) got right to the heart of the matter. It quickly explained that the LORD formed *adam* from *adamah*, the Hebrew word for ground. This is part of the unique story of monotheism. Israel's neighbors had their own creation stories about how the gods created people through fertility, but the Yahwist shared the

A Natural History of Scripture

creation of people as a process coming from the dust of the ground. Then the LORD "breathed into his nostrils the breath of life; and the man became a living being" (Genesis 2:7). This expressed the theological truth that the source of life is utterly dependent upon the one God.

Next the LORD put the man into a garden, which "should not really be surprising, since the notions of paradise and a garden of God are familiar themes in the literature of the biblical world."[20] Although the phrase "garden of God" did not show up in the Yahwist creation story, it did show up later in the Hebrew Scriptures (Ezekiel 28:13; 31:8-9). The Yahwist's exclusion of the phrase revealed his bias that the stories of monotheism are not about God or us, they are about our relationship with God. That is why they did not call it 'The Garden of God' or 'The Garden of Humans,' they called it "a garden in Eden" (Genesis 2:8).

Then the LORD grew "the tree of life also in the midst of the garden, and the tree of the knowledge of good and evil" (Genesis 2:9). The tree of life represented immortality and was "a motif widespread throughout the Ancient Near East that played an important role in Mesopotamian myth;"[21] the tree of knowledge was a unique addition from monotheism. Israel's ancient neighbors were obsessed with immortality, so by

> relegating the 'tree of life' to an insignificant, subordinate role in the Garden of Eden story, the Bible dissociates itself completely from this preoccupation. Its concern is with the issues of living rather than the question of death, with morality rather than mortality. Its problem is

not the mythical pursuit of eternity, but the actual relationship between man and God, the tension between the plans of God and the free-will of man.[22]

Finally, the LORD said, "It is not good that the man should be alone; I will make him a helper as his partner" (Genesis 2:18). The Hebrew word translated here as helper implies mutuality and interdependence rather than subordination. Indeed, one can even find God taking on this positive role of helper (Psalm 121:1-2). The Yahwist went on to say that the LORD "caused a deep sleep to fall upon the man, and he slept; then he took one of his ribs and closed up its place with flesh. And the rib that the LORD God had taken from the man he made into a woman" (Genesis 2:21-22). The woman's coming from the rib of the man entails no more subordination to the man than the man's coming from the dust of the ground implies his subordination to the ground.

The Flood

Later editors mixed two different oral stories of the flood to produce the story we have today. Separating out the Yahwist's version eliminates conflicting details and probably went something like this:

The LORD saw that the wickedness of humankind was great in the earth, and that every inclination of the thoughts of their hearts was only

A Natural History of Scripture

evil continually. And the LORD was sorry that he had made humankind on the earth, and it grieved him to his heart. So the LORD said, 'I will blot out from the earth the human beings I have created—people together with animals and creeping things and birds of the air, for I am sorry that I have made them.' But Noah found favor in the sight of the LORD (Genesis 6:5-8).

Then the LORD said to Noah, 'Go into the ark, you and all your household, for I have seen that you alone are righteous before me in this generation. Take with you seven pairs of all clean animals, the male and its mate; and a pair of the animals that are not clean, the male and its mate; and seven pairs of the birds of the air also, male and female, to keep their kind alive on the face of all the earth. For in seven days I will send rain on the earth for forty days and forty nights; and every living thing that I have made I will blot out from the face of the ground.' And Noah did all that the LORD had commanded him (Genesis 7:1-5).

And Noah with his sons and his wife and his sons' wives went into the ark to escape the waters of the flood. And after seven days the waters of the flood came on the earth. The rain fell on the earth forty days and forty nights, and the LORD shut him in (Genesis 7:7, 10, 12, 16b).

The flood continued forty days on the earth; and the waters increased, and bore up the ark, and

A Natural History of Scripture

it rose high above the earth. The waters swelled and increased greatly on the earth; and the ark floated on the face of the waters. The waters swelled so mightily on the earth that all the high mountains under the whole heaven were covered; the waters swelled above the mountains, covering them fifteen cubits deep...Everything on dry land in whose nostrils was the breath of life died. He blotted out every living thing that was on the face of the ground, human beings and animals and creeping things and birds of the air; they were blotted out from the earth. Only Noah was left, and those that were with him in the ark (Genesis 7:17-20, 22-23).

      The rain from the heavens was restrained, and the waters gradually receded from the earth...At the end of forty days Noah opened the windows of the ark that he had made...Then he sent out the dove from him, to see if the waters had subsided from the face of the ground; but the dove found no place to set its foot, and it returned to him to the ark, for the waters were still on the face of the whole earth. So he put out his hand and took it and brought it into the ark with him. He waited another seven days, and again he sent out the dove from the ark; and the dove came back to him in the evening, and there in its beak was a freshly plucked olive leaf; so Noah knew that the waters had subsided from the earth. Then he waited another seven days, and sent out the dove; and it did not return to him any more (Genesis 8:2b-3a, 6, 8-12).

A Natural History of Scripture

And Noah removed the covering of the ark, and looked, and saw that the face of the ground was drying...Then Noah built an altar to the LORD, and took of every clean animal and of every clean bird, and offered burnt offerings on the altar. And when the LORD smelled the pleasing odor, the LORD said in his heart, "I will never again curse the ground because of humankind, for the inclination of the human heart is evil from youth; nor will I ever again destroy every living creature as I have done. As long as the earth endures, seedtime and harvest, cold and heat, summer and winter, day and night, shall not cease" (Genesis 8:13b, 20-22).

The Rest of the Story

The stories of creation and flood give the flavor of the Yahwist's storytelling style. We know that his work can also be seen in many other parts of Israel's primeval stories reported in Genesis 1-11, as well as the stories of the patriarchs in Genesis 12-50. We also know that his style can be detected in several of the stories in the books of Exodus and Numbers. What we don't know is where the story ends, because there is no scholarly consensus on that very debatable topic. Some proposals for the location of the end of the Yahwist source include Numbers 14:8a, Joshua 11, Joshua 24, Judges 1:26, 1 Kings 2, 1 Kings 12, and 1 Kings 14:25.[23]

Let's take a short break for
Guided Exercise #2 on the next page.

A Natural History of Scripture

Guided Exercise #2

The choice of Saul to be king is reported in two different stories in 1 Samuel. The story comes from a combination of chapters 8:1-22 and 10:17-27. The other story can be found in chapter 9:1-10:16. Turn to that other story in a New Revised Standard Version of the Bible and look at the following differences to see how these three chapters combine two different oral stories into one written account.

1. Saul doesn't seem to know Samuel, referring to him simply as "the man of God" (9:7), rather than the judge of Israel (7:15; 8:1) whom all would surely have known.

2. This version is probably older than the other, because the term "seer" has gone out of use (9:9). The footnote also mentions this is a later comment that has been edited in.

3. Kingship is presented as a blessing that God decides to give (9:16) rather than a giving in to the people's demands (8:7). Different storytellers see things differently.

4. Samuel seems pleased with the idea of kingship (9:19) rather than displeased (8:6).

5. Samuel anoints Saul as king (10:1) rather than Saul being chosen as king by lot (10:21). Traditional attempts to harmonize this say it is a public and private account of the selection.

A Natural History of Scripture

Now we will return to the story of how the Bible came together. We will first reset the historical setting, then consider the next four documents to appear. Remember, at this time the Yahwist source was the only written document in the process of biblical composition.

Civil War

After Solomon's death, his son Rehoboam became king. The Israelites were supportive, but they were also concerned with the labor-intensive building programs of his father. The construction of the temple itself was too reminiscent of their time in Egypt, so they said, "Your father made our yoke heavy. Now therefore lighten the hard service of your father and his heavy yoke that he placed on us, and we will serve you" (1 Kings 12:4).

Rehoboam chose to be even harsher with the people, so they seceded. He remained the king over his native tribe of Judah and the neighboring tribe of Benjamin. The other tribes formed their own kingdom and appointed Jeroboam as their king. The formerly united monarchy quickly became a divided monarchy, with the Israelite settlement in the northern kingdom and Judah in the southern kingdom. Not wanting the ten tribes of his new kingdom to worship in Jerusalem, Jeroboam erected two temples outfitted with golden calves, and "this thing became a sin, for the people went to worship before the one at Bethel and before the other as far as Dan" (1 Kings 12:30).

A Natural History of Scripture

Rehoboam was so angry he assembled a mighty force to reunite the kingdom by coercion. They were turned back when the LORD said to them through a prophet "You shall not go up or fight against your kindred the people of Israel. Let everyone go home, for this thing is from me" (1 Kings 12:24). Unfortunately, the Judahites did no better than the Israelites, by building idolatrous temples. In fact, the writer of this material even said they "committed all the abominations of the nations that the LORD drove out before the people of Israel" (1 Kings 14:24). *The chart on the next page lists all of the kings of Israel and Judah, along with their regnal years.*[24]

The Court Narrative

Rehoboam's court had a writer who probably studied under the Yahwist, and now that the kingdom was divided, it was time to record the story of King David. This account can be found between 2 Samuel 9 and 1 Kings 1. A current author has been able to detach the story from its surroundings and present it on its own terms.[25] The story is referred to as the Court Narrative and falls into place as the second Hebrew text. The third through fifth written texts will also appear during this time, which will ultimately bring us to the exile where much of the editing stage began. The constant threat of violence between the two kingdoms provided the motivation to assure that the sacred stories would live on by getting them written down.

A Natural History of Scripture

The Northern and Southern Kings

Israelite Kings	Years	Judahite Kings	Years
Jeroboam I	922-901	Rehoboam	922-915
Nadab	901-900	Abijam	915-913
Baasha	900-877	Asa	913-873
Elah	877-876	Jehoshaphat	873-849
Zimri	876	Jehoram	849-842
Omri	876-869	Ahaziah	842
Ahab	869-850	Athaliah (queen)	842-837
Ahaziah	850-849	Jehoash	837-800
Joram	849-842	Amaziah	800-783
Jehu	842-815	Uzziah	783-742
Jehoahaz	815-801	Jotham	742-735
Joash	801-786	Ahaz	735-715
Jeroboam II	786-746	Hezekiah	715-687
Zechariah	746	Manasseh	687-642
Shallum	745	Amon	642-640
Menahem	745-738	Josiah	640-609
Pekahiah	737-732	Jehoahaz II	609
Pekah	732-732	Jehoiakim	609-598
Hoshea	732-722	Jehoiachin	598
		Zedekiah	597-586

Figure 1

A Natural History of Scripture

The Elohist Source

Just as the Yahwists preferred to use the word *Yahweh* for God, an individual or group of people who preferred to use the word *Elohim* for God wrote what is now referred to as the Elohist source. The purpose of the Elohist source was to revise the story of Israel's beginnings from the vantage of the northern kingdom of Israel. The first vision of Israel's beginnings was in the Yahwist source, written a century earlier in what became the southern kingdom of Judah. Scholars now believe that we only have part of the Elohist source because later Judahite editors gave preference to their own version of Israel's beginnings. The Elohists typically wrote about divine revelations occurring in dreams and emphasized the fear of God.

The Patriarchs

The Elohists started their story with Abraham passing off his wife as his sister (Genesis 20:1-18). This was a revision of the Yahwist's account, which can be found in Genesis 12:10-20. The next revision was the story of Hagar and Ishmael (Genesis 21:8-21), through whom the Muslims trace their covenantal promise of land to Abraham. The Yahwist version can be found in Genesis 16:4-14. Another Elohist revision was that of Abraham and Abimelech (Genesis 21:22-34), which can be found in its Yahwist version in Genesis 26:26-33. This can serve as an informal guided exercise by looking up and comparing each of these accounts.

A Natural History of Scripture

The story of the binding of Isaac (Genesis 22:1-4) would be lost if the Judahite editors had not liked it, because the Yahwists did not record it. Jacob's ladder dream (Genesis 28:10-22) was a skillfully edited mix of Elohist and Yahwist sources, while the story of Jacob being named Israel (Genesis 32:22-30) was notably missing from the Yahwist's story.

The story of Joseph and his brothers (Genesis 37) was again an artful editing of the two sources, while Joseph's dream interpretations in Genesis 40-41 were an Elohist addition. The stories of Joseph's brothers in Egypt in Genesis 42-45 continued the blending work of a later editor, as well as the concluding stories of Jacob in Egypt in Genesis 46-50. The text we have today represents a final editing that often preserved stories that different groups wanted to forget.

Moses

Most of Exodus 5-13 came from the Elohists, while the sea crossing was an edited mix of stories. Teasing out the Elohist source gives a very different story at the *yam suf* (Sea of Reeds)[26] than the story reported in Chapter 1 (under the subhead *The First Oral Library*). The Elohist source might have originally gone something like this:

> The angel of God who was going before the Israelite army moved and went behind them. It came between the army of Egypt and the army of Israel. He clogged their chariot wheels so that they turned with difficulty. Then the prophet Miriam, Aaron's sister, took a tambourine in her hand; and all the

A Natural History of Scripture

women went out after her with tambourines and with dancing. And Miriam sang to them; 'Sing to the LORD, for he has triumphed gloriously; horse and rider he has thrown into the sea' (Exodus 14:19a, 20a, 25a; 15:20-21).

The Charlton Heston movie of Moses parting the Red Sea was great Hollywood stuff, but it was based on the grandeur of the Yahwist source. The Elohist source simply had the Egyptians drive their chariots into a muddy swamp and get stuck in the rising tide. The reason we have both versions preserved is a tribute to the inclusive graciousness of the ancient editors. Perhaps the monotheistic religions of today could learn something useful about inclusiveness when it comes to our exclusive theologies.

The Rest of the Story

A covenant ceremony was preserved in both sources. The Elohist source appeared in Exodus 24:1-2, 9-11 and the Yahwist source appeared in the intervening verses of 3-8. The story of the golden calf (Exodus 32:1-33:11) appeared only in the Elohist source, which made sense because it would play a role later in the story of the northern kingdom. The Elohists also added the stories of Moses' Cushite wife (Numbers 12:1-16), Balak and Balaam (Numbers 22:2-24:25), the appointment of Joshua (Deuteronomy 31:14-15, 23), and the death of Moses (Deuteronomy 34:1-12).

A Natural History of Scripture

The Deuteronomic Source

Some people today believe that the Bible is a relic and has nothing to do with today. The Judahites faced the same problem but came up with a different answer. Rather than discarding the five hundred-year-old laws that came from God to Moses on Mount Sinai, an individual or group of people wrote the book of Deuteronomy as a means of revising the ancient laws to fit their times. While this revision made the book secondary, it also added to the law: "These are the words of the covenant that the LORD commanded Moses to make with the Israelites in the land of Moab, in addition to the covenant that he made with them at Horeb" (Deuteronomy 29:1).

Deuteronomy was presented as a farewell speech delivered by Moses. It was sermonic in style, reminding Moses' successors of the values of their culture, but the sermons "are filled with emphases and concerns that developed long after the time of Moses."[27] Although the book appears to stand well on its own, it is obviously a composite work. Most scholars today believe that the original book consisted of chapters 4:44—28:68, with later added introductory and supplementary material.

The Deuteronomistic History

Let's keep track. Four Hebrew texts were in existence by the mid-seventh century BC:

A Natural History of Scripture

     1) *the Yahwist source*, written during the united monarchy in Jerusalem, covering the early history of the nation;
     2) *the Court Narrative*, written during the divided monarchy in Judah, covering the life of King David;
     3) *the Elohist source*, written during the divided monarchy in Israel, covering the early history of the nation from the perspective of the northern kingdom, and
     4) *the Deuteronomic source*, written during the divided monarchy in Judah, covering a reinterpretation of the laws given during the exodus and calling for a centralization of worship in Jerusalem.

Four Hebrew prophets (Amos, Hosea, Isaiah 1-39, and Micah) had also completed their prophecies by this time, but the material was to go through several stages of editing before they came to look like they do now.

     The Deuteronomistic History became the fifth written work. An individual or group of people recorded the oral stories that became the books of Joshua, Judges, Samuel, and Kings. Joshua was the result of the stories about settling the promised land. Judges put into writing the various stories about tribal heroes in an effort to bring community out of diversity. Samuel was about the founding of Israel's monarchy, and Kings was about the fall of the kingdoms. This brought an end to the enterprise of writing about God's revelation in the form of law. The various and separate documents would wait three hundred years before finding cohesiveness and unity.

A Natural History of Scripture

This would come from the fall of the northern and southern kingdoms, and the advent of exile. Meanwhile, the age of prophets was ready to burst onto the stage, bringing with them a new form of revelation. Gloom and doom would be the order of the day, as individual prophets attempted to bring God's people back in line with obedience to the law.

A Natural History of Scripture

Chapter 3
Prophets: First Branch of a New Species

Prenatal Stage: Storytellers	Infant Stage: Writers	Adolescent Stage: Editors				Adult Stage: Standardizers	
Oral History	Written History	**Pro-phets**	Priests	Trans-lators	Evan-gelists	Politi-cians	Pub-lishers

2000 BC   950 BC   750 BC 586 BC   332 BC   63 BC   AD 144   AD 1454   NOW

They were denouncers of the present rather than foretellers of the future.[28]

As law ended and prophecy began, the moral fiber of the divided monarchy was frayed. To make things worse, marauding empires were threatening from the north. It was time for a new revelation from God, and the medium of prophecy stepped up to the challenge. Before looking at the prophets in their proper historical context, we will pause for a short update of people and events leading to this unique time in history.

A Natural History of Scripture

Background

Elijah and Elisha

Unfortunately, there is no book of the prophet Elijah, but the oral tradition has been preserved in 1 and 2 Kings. Elijah spent much of his time railing against polytheistic worship in Israel. To prove to King Ahab that the one God of Israel controlled the rain, rather than the old Canaanite god Baal, he declared "As the LORD God of Israel lives, before whom I stand, there shall be neither dew nor rain these years, except by my word" (1 Kings 17:1). After three years of drought, the LORD told Elijah to return to Ahab. At Mount Carmel, Elijah challenged Ahab's prophets of Baal to a competition. Elijah and the LORD were victorious and the prophets of Baal were killed. When Ahab's wife Jezebel heard what Elijah had done, she ordered his immediate death. Elijah fled for his life to Mount Horeb where the LORD instructed him to return and "anoint Elisha son of Shaphat of Abel-meholah as prophet in your place" (1 Kings 19:16).

In keeping with the ancient writer's method of showing greatness in terms of miracles, Elijah and Elisha arrived at the Jordan river and experienced yet another division of water and crossing on dry ground (2 Kings 2:8). As they talked on the other side, "a chariot of fire and horses of fire separated the two of them, and Elijah ascended in a whirlwind into heaven" (2 Kings 2:11). Elisha picked up Elijah's mantle and then demonstrated the continuation of power by parting the waters of the Jordan and returning.

A Natural History of Scripture

After performing many miracles, Elisha reached out to a non-Israelite. We are told that Naaman, the commander of Syria's army, suffered from leprosy. Elisha sent word to Naaman to "wash in the Jordan seven times, and your flesh shall be restored and you shall be clean" (2 Kings 5:10). After a bit of fussing, Naaman followed Elisha's words and was healed. He became an instant convert to monotheism, went to Elisha and said, "Now I know that there is no god in all the earth except in Israel" (2 Kings 5:15).

Elisha then sent a disciple to anoint Jehu as the next king over Israel. Jehu proceeded to kill King Joram, his mother Jezebel, all of Ahab's descendents and officers, and the prophets and worshippers of Baal. We are then shockingly told that the LORD was pleased with Jehu's work: "Because you have done well in carrying out what I consider right, and in accordance with all that was in my heart have dealt with the house of Ahab, your sons of the fourth generation shall sit on the throne of Israel" (2 Kings 10:30). While we respect the sanctity of God's Word, I hope it helps to see the Bible as a very human composition, rather than God's words.

Unfortunately neither Jehu nor his reigning sons turned aside from Baal worship and Israel slowly weakened. After Elisha's death, a concluding miracle story said that a dead man "was thrown into the grave of Elisha; as soon as the man touched the bones of Elisha, he came to life and stood on his feet" (2 Kings 13:21). Are we to believe these stories as literal history? They probably follow a historical storyline, but the stories served a purpose. They shared the author's sense of the awesomeness of God.

A Natural History of Scripture

Ninth Century Kings

As we continue through the story of bibliogenesis and evolution, the next bit of history again comes from the oral stage. What this teaches us is that the oral stage was dramatically important in the development of the Bible. Rehoboam's grandson Asa was the third king of Judah and he reigned forty-one years in Jerusalem. Although he was continually at war with Israel, his plaudits came because he "put away the male temple prostitutes out of the land, and removed all the idols that his ancestors had made" (1 Kings 15:12). Asa's son Jehoshaphat reigned twenty-five years in Jerusalem and followed in his father's footsteps with further reform (1 Kings 22:46).

Jehosaphat's son Jehoram succeeded him, who was succeeded by his son Ahaziah (2 Kings 8:24). Ahaziah was murdered the same year he took the throne, which was seized by Jehoram's widow Athaliah. After the murder of Athaliah, Jehoash took over and reigned as king for forty years. He was the grandson of Athaliah and "was only seven years old when he began to reign" (2 Kings 11:21).

Amos and Hosea

By this time the written word was making progress in the northern kingdom. The Elohists had written their revision of the southern kingdom's version of Israel's beginnings, and now there were oral stories of prophets. Perhaps the remaining prophets or their disciples were motivated by the

A Natural History of Scripture

desire to have their message live on, so they started recording their works in scrolls bearing the author's name.

This time was a period of great prosperity and national confidence, as Assyria overthrew Syria and weak kings were left in charge. It was also a time when sharp divisions in Israelite wealth first appeared and religion became corrupt. In light of all this, it was time to reflect on what God might have to say. Amos and Hosea accepted this task and became known as spokesmen for God. While their prophecies took place in the time frames noted, it was much later that their stories were written down.

Amos

The royal sanctuary at Bethel was where Amos chose to unleash the full power of his message. In a classic confrontation with the official priest of Bethel (Amos 7:10-17), Amos refused to flee to Judah and prophesy there. His message was gloom and doom precisely because of Israel's status. The popular sentiment of the day was that their special status as God's people gave them assurance of forgiveness, but Amos proclaimed that their special status gave them responsibility, which held them to higher standards.

Amos most notably attacked Israelite worship because it was empty when unaccompanied by ethical behavior. Speaking in God's name he said "I hate, I despise your festivals, and I take no delight in your solemn assemblies" (Amos 5:21). Amos did not just name the problems, he offered a solution: "But let justice roll down like waters, and righteousness like an everflowing stream" (Amos 5:24).

A Natural History of Scripture

Hosea

While Amos spoke to the Israelites as an angry Judahite from the southern kingdom, Hosea was speaking to his own people. He was a compassionate man who loved his people and was aware of their sin. To symbolize Israel's unfaithful relationship with God, the LORD told Hosea to "Go, take for yourself a wife of whoredom and have children of whoredom, for the land commits great whoredom by forsaking the LORD"(Hosea 1:2).

Rather than offering a solution like Amos, Hosea lived an example of redeeming love. He married Gomer, became repeatedly rejected, and always took back his unfaithful wife. He used the husband/wife metaphor for the God/Israel relationship, but in the end Hosea mournfully prophesied that "Because they have not listened to him, my God will reject them; they shall become wanderers among the nations" (Hosea 9:17).

Isaiah 1-39

Judah was uniquely open to the counsel of prophets, but the counsel was not always what the kings wanted to hear. Isaiah was a prophet from the capital city of Jerusalem, possibly of noble descent, who proclaimed his message to Judah and Jerusalem. Micah was a commoner who was a prophet from the village of Moresheth. The prophets are discussed here in their proper historical context, but their work was not

A Natural History of Scripture

recorded until later. Focusing on the background serves the purpose of keeping us from misunderstanding the text.

The first thirty-nine chapters of Isaiah mostly contain his work, while the remaining chapters are post-exilic. Although Isaiah preached a word of gloom and doom, he also held out hope. Isaiah prophesied about an age of peace when nations "shall beat their swords into plowshares, and their spears into pruning hooks; nation shall not lift up sword against nation, neither shall they learn war any more" (Isaiah 2:4).

Isaiah also held out hope for an ideal king, so he told King Ahaz that there was already a sign: "Look, the young woman is with child and shall bear a son, and shall name him Immanuel" (Isaiah 7:14). Isaiah probably had Hezekiah in mind when he described how this child would become their ideal king: "For a child has been born for us, a son given to us; authority rests upon his shoulders; and he is named Wonderful Counselor, Mighty God, Everlasting Father, Prince of Peace" (Isaiah 9:6).

Isaiah continued to describe how this ideal king would rule: "The spirit of the LORD shall rest on him, the spirit of wisdom and understanding, the spirit of counsel and might, the spirit of knowledge and the fear of the LORD" (Isaiah 11:2). Toward the end of Isaiah's work, King Hezekiah is indeed on the throne but in ill health. The LORD told Isaiah to:

> Go and say to Hezekiah, Thus says the LORD, the God of your ancestor David: I have heard your prayer, I have seen your tears; I will add fifteen years to your life. I will deliver you and this city out of the hand of the king of Assyria, and defend this city. 'This is the sign to you from the

A Natural History of Scripture

LORD, that the LORD will do this thing that he has promised: See, I will make the shadow cast by the declining sun on the dial of Ahaz turn back ten steps.' So the sun turned back on the dial the ten steps by which it had declined" (Isaiah 38:5-8).

*Take a moment now to look at
Guided Exercise #3 on the next page.*

Micah

Micah was remembered by a later prophet (Jeremiah 26:18) for his unique prophecy of the fall of Jerusalem and the destruction of the temple. Micah said "Therefore because of you Zion shall be plowed as a field; Jerusalem shall become a heap of ruins, and the mountain of the house a wooded height" (Micah 3:12). However, he did not just name a problem, he also offered a solution: "He has told you, O mortal, what is good; and what does the LORD require of you but to do justice, and to love kindness, and to walk humbly with your God?" (Micah 6:8).

This last verse is familiar to most Christians, but the context is what gives it power. Micah was a commoner speaking to the capital city. This reminds me of the 'Cutters' bicycle team taking on the fraternity teams in the movie Breaking Away. Isn't it difficult to take people serious when we look down our nose at them? Micah was also speaking at the edge of Israel's demise. This reminds me of Christians who proclaim that the end is coming soon, so we better turn

A Natural History of Scripture

Guided Exercise #3

The present can learn from the past, such as our mistakes, but the past cannot learn from the present. While this principle seems self-evident, look what happens when we apply it to the Bible: we can learn about the New Testament from the Old Testament, but we cannot learn about the Old Testament from the New Testament. This helps us to properly interpret the Old Testament. Look at some commonly misunderstood Isaiah texts.

1. Isaiah 7:14—Christians hear this text each year as they celebrate Christmas. The principle teaches us that it is okay to see Jesus as a sign, given from the Lord, who became "Immanuel", but it is not okay to say that this text was a prophecy about Jesus.
2. Isaiah 9:6—same situation. While Jesus can be understood as fulfilling this prophecy, it is about a king who is soon to arrive in 8th century BC Israel.
3. Isaiah 11:2—this text is about the Messiah, whom the Israelites expected to be a human. It embodies characteristics of the best Hebrew kings of the past.
4. Isaiah 14:12—if you like the book of Revelation, you are probably familiar with this text. However, it is about the king of Babylon (see verse 4). Christian fantasy has run wild because when Saint Jerome translated "Day Star" into Latin he used the words for light-bearer, which are *lux-ifer*, which was written as *Lucifer*.

A Natural History of Scripture

our lives around. Isn't it difficult to practice justice, kindness, and humility when a tornado is in the forecast?

The Fall of Israel to the Assyrians

The northern kingdom of Israel only lasted two hundred years. During this time, the northerners established Samaria as their capital, but by the late eighth century BC it was ruled by Assyria. When Assyria's king Tiglath-Pileser died, Israel's king Hoshea rebelled and after a three year siege, the king of Assyria captured Samaria and deported the Israelites (2 Kings 17:6). *This ended the kingdom of Israel, and from that time on the land was known as Samaria instead of Israel (2 Kings 17:24) and its inhabitants were known as Samaritans instead of Israelites.*

Hezekiah's Reform

This was a unique time in the land of Judah. Israel had recently fallen, leaving Judah as the only independent state in the area, and the Assyrian Empire was dealing with dissension from Babylon. With the empire's attention diverted, Hezekiah conducted religious reform when he "removed the high places, broke down the pillars, and cut down the sacred pole. He broke in pieces the bronze serpent that Moses had made, for until those days the people of Israel had made offerings to it; it was called Nehushtan" (2 Kings 18:4).

A Natural History of Scripture

When the Assyrian monarch Sargon II died, Sennacherib ascended the throne. This vulnerable time of transition proved difficult for Sennacherib because he was challenged from both Babylon and Egypt. Hezekiah joined the revolt and was dealt a crushing defeat (2 Kings 18:13), but Jerusalem was spared because an "angel of the LORD set out and struck down one hundred eighty-five thousand in the camp of the Assyrians" (2 Kings 19:35). Although Jerusalem was spared, Judah would remain under the shadow of the Assyrian Empire for its remaining years.

Zephaniah and Jeremiah

Zephaniah

This time in history brings our focus back to the prophets. Just as the historical setting was the main thing effecting biblical formation when dealing with the oral stage, so also the historical setting was the main thing effecting biblical formation when dealing with the writing stage. The historical importance about Zephaniah was his role as a prophet during the reign of King Josiah, and the fact that he was the grandson of King Hezekiah (Zephaniah 1:1).

Zephaniah followed in the same line of thought as his eighth century predecessors, Isaiah and Micah. He prophesied against the people of Judah for blending their worship of the LORD with elements of their neighboring state's religions. He threatened that the LORD would destroy them for their

A Natural History of Scripture

idolatrous worship, and told them: "Seek the LORD, all you humble of the land, who do his commands; seek righteousness, seek humility; perhaps you may be hidden on the day of the LORD's wrath" (Zephaniah 2:3).

Zephaniah had given up on the hierarchy of the day and turned his attention to preparing the humble so they might avoid God's vengeance. One might think that his own royal lineage would give him a chance to be heard by aristocracy, but it seems that his efforts went unheeded. Perhaps he did the work of planting seeds, because some fourteen years later sweeping religious reforms would be successful.

Jeremiah

Jeremiah prophesied from the time of King Josiah to the fall of Jerusalem. His work contained the first explicit reference to written Hebrew when the LORD said, "Take a scroll and write on it all the words that I have spoken to you against Israel and Judah and all the nations, from the day I spoke to you, from the days of Josiah until today" (Jeremiah 36:2). His work also contained his personal spiritual struggles with God. He complained that the LORD called him to his difficult task: "But I was like a gentle lamb led to the slaughter" (Jeremiah 11:19).

Jeremiah has been called the weeping prophet because he was unfortunate enough to see the fulfillment of his dire prophecies. His work could be summarized by the following statement about Judah's rejection of the living God and acceptance of the false gods: "for my people have

A Natural History of Scripture

committed two evils: they have forsaken me, the fountain of living water, and dug out cisterns for themselves, cracked cisterns that can hold no water" (Jeremiah 2:13).

Josiah's Reform

Josiah ascended the throne at the tender age of eight, due to the assassination of his father. He reigned from 640 BC—609 BC and was declared the greatest king in biblical history, which was no small achievement considering his grandfather King Manasseh, his father King Amon, and his son King Jehoiakim were evil. Josiah had some Bill Clinton-like luck in him because he proved to be the right person at the right time. As he grew up, Assyria lost control of its empire, bringing discredit to its gods.

The scene was ripe for reform when in 621 BC the High Priest Hilkiah "found the book of the law in the house of the LORD" (2 Kings 22:8). The discovery of this book had great importance on the future of the people of Israel. What was probably found was the original part of the book of Deuteronomy and it spurred King Josiah to enact sweeping reforms. This was a great learning for me personally, because it set the stage for Judaism to proceed from a revision of the laws rather than the original laws. This would continue to be the case much later on as Judaism would focus more on an interpretation of the law (the Talmud) rather than the original laws. The same would also hold true for Christianity as it would find itself later on focusing more on an interpretation of the gospels (Paul's Epistles) rather than the original gospels.

A Natural History of Scripture

Getting back to King Josiah, he called all the people to the temple and

> read in their hearing all the words of the book of the covenant that had been found in the house of the LORD. The king stood by the pillar and made a covenant before the LORD, to follow the LORD, keeping his commandments, his decrees, and his statutes, with all his heart and all his soul, to perform the words of this covenant that were written in this book. All the people joined in the covenant (2 Kings 23:2-3).

Habbakuk, Nahum, and Ezekiel 1-32

Habbakuk

Just as the oral stage was so important in the development of what became the Law section of the Hebrew Scriptures, the writing stage was of great importance in the development of the eventual Prophets section of the Hebrew Scriptures. Habbakuk was a prophet who questioned God's justice when he asked "O LORD, how long shall I cry for help, and you will not listen? Or cry to you 'Violence!' and you will not save?" (Habakkuk 1:2). He was upset that the LORD chose the faithless Babylonians to persecute the righteous Judahites, so he argued that "Your eyes are too pure to

A Natural History of Scripture

behold evil, and you cannot look on wrongdoing; why do you look on the treacherous, and are silent when the wicked swallow those more righteous than they?" (Habakkuk 1:13).

Habakkuk answered his own question when he said, "Look at the proud! Their spirit is not right in them, but the righteous live by their faith" (Habakkuk 2:4). He then gave a vision of hope for the future by quoting from Isaiah 11:9, "But the earth will be filled with the knowledge of the glory of the LORD, as the waters cover the sea" (Habakkuk 2:14). *We have now reached a point in time where scripture is starting to be quoted in scripture.* This gives a sense that the community was beginning to accept particular scrolls, paving the way for the eventual agreement on which scrolls to accept as part of the finalized Hebrew Scriptures.

Nahum

I like Nahum because you know where you stand with him. Other than that he is a little hard to take. The book of Nahum is a poetic celebration over the destruction of Nineveh, the capital of Assyria. Who in their right mind waxes poetic over the downfall of others? Then again war usually produces that response and Holy War adds the dimension of having God on your side. Nahum begins his work by saying that "A jealous and avenging God is the LORD, the LORD is avenging and wrathful; the LORD takes vengeance on his adversaries and rages against his enemies" (Nahum 1:2). Somehow I get

A Natural History of Scripture

a feeling that Nahum is the one raging against his enemies here.

Surprisingly he seemed to be myopic about the divine judgment against Judah, who itself had become an enemy of the LORD. Perhaps this isn't so surprising because blame rarely looks inward. I once served a church that had a history of running their pastors out because they were incapable of considering themselves to be part of their problems. Staying true to form, Nahum closed his work with hatred against Nineveh by saying "There is no assuaging your hurt, your wound is mortal. All who hear the news about you clap their hands over you. For who has ever escaped your endless cruelty?" (Nahum 3:19).

Ezekiel 1-32

Ezekiel was a prophet before and after the fall of Jerusalem, making his work important in the transition from preexilic to postexilic faith. Chapters 1-24 contain prophecies against Israel and chapters 25-32 contain prophecies against foreign powers. We will deal with chapters 33-48 in the next chapter. The purpose of Ezekiel's work, prior to the fall of Jerusalem, was to explain why God was preparing to reject the covenant of land through the upcoming exile. This was an important task because the people believed that God would never break the covenant.

Ezekiel's task was to explain that they were the ones breaking the covenant. His prophecy said that Jerusalem "has wickedly rebelled against my ordinances more than the nations, and against my statutes more than the countries round about her, by rejecting my ordinances and not walking in my statutes. Therefore thus says the Lord God: Because you are more turbulent than the nations that are round about you, and have not walked in my statutes or kept my ordinances, but have acted according to the ordinances of the nations that are round about you; therefore thus says the Lord God: Behold, I, even I, am against you; and I will execute judgments in the midst of you in the sight of the nations" (Ezekiel 5:6-8).

The Fall of Judah to the Babylonians

In the closing decade of Judah's life, King Zedekiah was encouraged because Egypt's King Apries was an ally and was on the move up the Mediterranean coast. That's when King Zedekiah made a fateful decision to renounce any allegiance to Babylon. Babylon's King Nebuchadnezzar responded by marching his troops into Jerusalem, withdrawing upon the arrival of the Egyptian army (Jeremiah 37:11). After the Egyptians departed, the Babylonians resumed their siege.

The siege of Jerusalem was horrendous. It lasted two years, while the people within its walls slowly died of hunger and thirst. One night King Zedekiah decided to flee, but

> the army of the Chaldeans pursued the king, and overtook him in the plains of Jericho; all his army was scattered, deserting him. Then they captured the king and brought him up to the king of Babylon at Riblah, who passed sentence on him. They slaughtered the sons of Zedekiah before

A Natural History of Scripture

his eyes, then put out the eyes of Zedekiah; they bound him in fetters and took him to Babylon (2 Kings 25:5-7).

Judah had lasted four hundred years and the Judahites believed they were invincible. The loss to Nebuchadnezzar in 586 BC was devastating because God had chosen both Jerusalem and the ancestors of David to rule over the city. They also had God's temple in their midst, but Jeremiah had cautioned "Do not trust in these deceptive words: 'This is the temple of the LORD'" (Jeremiah 7:4).

Destruction of the First Temple

It must have been beyond words for the Judahites to watch God's temple burn. The captain of Nebuchadnezzar's bodyguards "burned the house of the LORD, the king's house, and all the houses of Jerusalem" (2 Kings 25:9). The Babylonians left some of the poorest people of the land, had the remaining leaders executed, and "took into exile from Jerusalem eight hundred thirty-two persons" (Jeremiah 52:29). Jeremiah counseled the deportees to pray for Babylon—"for in its welfare you will find your welfare" (Jeremiah 29:7), and he prophesied for the LORD—"Only when Babylon's seventy years are completed will I visit you, and I will fulfill to you my promise and bring you back to this place" (Jeremiah 29:10).

A Natural History of Scripture

Part Three
Adolescent Stage: Editors

Prenatal Stage:	Infant Stage:			Adolescent Stage:			Adult Stage:	
Storytellers	Writers			Editors			Standardizers	
Oral History	Written History	Pro-phets	Priests	Trans-lators	Evan-gelists		Politi-cians	Pub-lishers

2000 BC   950 BC   750 BC   586 BC   332 BC   63 BC   AD 144   AD 1454   NOW

The great genius of the seventh century creators of this national epic was the way in which they wove the earlier stories together without stripping them of their humanity or individual distinctiveness.[29]

The Adolescent Stage explores the development of editors, products of inheritance, which is the third and final undeniable fact of natural selection. Darwin had no idea how inheritance worked, he simply noted that some of the variation would be inherited by the offspring. This was also a key factor in understanding biblical composition. Biblical scholars discovered that the various writings were mixed together by late editors, who produced material that

A Natural History of Scripture

inherited the features of the parent information. The developmental change in biblical words from writers to editors evolved three different canons of edited stories: priests, translators, and evangelists. They served the purpose of moving disparate writings toward a unified whole, which was an important step toward preservation.

The Dispersion from the promised land created a crisis for the Judahites. Their faith was plundered precisely because they no longer possessed their God-promised land. What carried the remnant through was the fact they were still God's people, no matter how tattered and distant that relationship seemed now. These people of God began as Hebrews through the trials of Abraham, Isaac, Jacob, and Joseph. Then they became Israelites under the leadership of Moses, Joshua, judges and kings. Next they were Judahites, as an expression of their identification with the southern kingdom of Judah, and as opposed to the ten tribes who seceded north and remained Israelites.

But who were they now? They could not very well be Judahites, because they no longer lived in Judah. So when they return from Babylon, they will become Jews. This will affirm their unity with the former southern kingdom of Judah, while acknowledging it is no longer under their control. Editors will use this time to unify the collection of Hebrew Scriptures, which will also symbolize the Judahites unification in their new beginning as Jews. It is into this setting that Chapter 4 begins. The exile in Babylon will prove to be a short prelude to Persian rule, which will last until Alexander the Great brings Hellenism into the ancient Near East.

A Natural History of Scripture

Chapter 4
Priests: Gradualism in Action

Prenatal Stage: Storytellers	Infant Stage: Writers		Adolescent Stage: Editors			Adult Stage: Standardizers	
Oral History	Written History	Pro- phets	Priests	Trans- lators	Evan- gelists	Politi- cians	Pub- lishers
2000 BC	950 BC	750 BC	586 BC	332 BC	63 BC	AD 144	AD 1454 NOW

So the experiment in living as the people of God under the laws of the covenant came to a tragic end.[30]

In the field of evolution, gradualism asserts unbroken historical connectedness between an organism and its descendants. In the evolution of the Bible, priests served the same purpose by connecting the disparate writings from the former kingdoms. Written by priests during the exile in Babylon, the Priestly source became the glue that united the first three writings. Later editors then used Deuteronomy as a hinge book to connect the edited writings to the Deuteronomistic History. The complete story of creation to

A Natural History of Scripture

exile was further edited and canonized as the story that shared the faith of the Hebrew people.

The Exile in Babylon

Little is known about life in Babylon during the exile. We do know that when Israel was conquered in 722 BC, the ten tribes were dispersed and lost. However, when Judah was conquered in 586 BC, the Judahites somehow managed to maintain their collective identity as God's people. One thing that helped was that the Judahites were not held in bondage as slaves like they were in Egypt. Even their former king was released from prison and treated well (Jeremiah 52:31-34). While there, many learned the Aramaic language of the Babylonians, which slowly replaced Hebrew and was still used during the time of Jesus.

This was also a time to study and preserve the sacred scrolls. The written stories of their faith were collected and edited and the preexilic prophecies that came true were elevated in importance. The major stumbling block had to do with understanding their two main theological truths: 1) God had promised them land, and 2) they were God's people. Some new theological truths were needed and that is what the exilic prophets offered. The rebuilding of Judahite faith was accomplished by taking the old stories of exodus (to promised land) and creation (as God's people), and making them symbols of the future. The new theological truths to be preached were simply new exodus and new creation (different but parallel to the old).

A Natural History of Scripture

Ezekiel 33-48 and Isaiah 40-66

This brings us to Ezekiel and the prophecies he shared during the exile. Chapters 33-39 prophesy a new exodus through departure to the promised land, and chapters 40-48 prophesy a new creation through the rebuilding of the Holy City. Ezekiel had a mission to revive hope that the people of Israel would return to their homeland. In his vision of a valley of dry bones coming to life, he spoke for the LORD: "I will put my spirit within you, and you shall live, and I will place you on your own soil; then you shall know that I, the LORD, have spoken and will act" (Ezekiel 37:14). Ezekiel then described the rebuilding of the city of Jerusalem and the temple, and continuing with symbolism, he announced "the name of the city from that time on shall be, The LORD is There" (Ezekiel 48:35).

An unknown prophet during the exile wrote what became Isaiah 40-55, and disciples of the unknown prophet wrote chapters 56-66 at some later time. This work began with "Comfort, O comfort my people, says your God. Speak tenderly to Jerusalem, and cry to her that she has served her term" (Isaiah 40:1-2). He then called upon his fellow exiled Hebrews using exodus imagery to build hope:

> Thus says the LORD, who makes a way in the sea, a path in the mighty waters, who brings out chariot and horse, army and warrior; they lie down, they cannot rise, they are extinguished, quenched like a wick: Do not remember the former things, or consider the things of old. I am about to do a new thing; now it springs forth, do you not perceive it? I

A Natural History of Scripture

will make a way in the wilderness and rivers in the desert (Isaiah 43:16-19).

Isaiah then prophesied that Cyrus, the king of Persia, would liberate them from exile: "Thus says the LORD to his anointed, to Cyrus, whose right hand I have grasped to subdue nations before him and strip kings of their robes, to open doors before him—and the gates shall not be closed" (Isaiah 45:1). Isaiah also gave them a new vision of their purpose as God's people. God was using the exiled remnants to redeem humanity to monotheism: "Surely he has borne our infirmities and carried our diseases; yet we accounted him stricken, struck down by God, and afflicted. But he was wounded for our transgressions, crushed for our iniquities; upon him was the punishment that made us whole, and by his bruises we are healed" (Isaiah 53:4-5).

See Guided Exercise #4 on the next page for further details.

The Fall of Babylon to the Persians

After Nebuchadnezzar died, Babylonian power declined. The new powerhouse who burst onto the scene was indeed King Cyrus of Persia. In the autumn of 539 BC, Cyrus and his troops marched into Babylon and easily overthrew it. King Cyrus soon declared an edict that said "The LORD, the God of heaven, has given me all the kingdoms of the earth, and he has charged me to build him a house at Jerusalem in Judah. Any of those among you who are of his people—may their God be with them!—are now permitted to go up to

A Natural History of Scripture

Guided Exercise #4

Isaiah 40-55 is known as Deutero-Isaiah, meaning second Isaiah. My first "ah-ha" experience with this book came when I discovered that the background of Isaiah 40-55 was 200 years later than the background of Isaiah 1-39. Our text today gives no hint of this. The end of Isaiah 39 mentions the eighth century king Hezekiah and the beginning of Isaiah 40 just seems to continue. Look at the following texts and see how context is important for understanding.

1. Isaiah 40:1-2—If we allow this text to remain in the eighth century BC, then what is the problem with Jerusalem? It wasn't to fall until 586 BC. When we discover Isaiah 40-55 was an anonymous exilic prophet prophesying Judah's return to Jersusalem, the "double for all her sins" makes sense.
2. Isaiah 44:24-28—This text even mentioned Cyrus as God's shepherd who had been called to carry out the divine will. Without placing this text in its proper historical context, it would be meaningless.
3. Isaiah 48:6-8—This text was about the new creation of God's people through the new exodus to the promised land. Cyrus was preparing to deliver Israel from exile and the prophet was telling the people to believe.
4. Isaiah 52:13-15—This text prophesied God's servant, the people of Israel, being lifted back up. The shocking fall of Jerusalem astonished many of the neighboring nations and kings.

A Natural History of Scripture

Jerusalem in Judah, and rebuild the house of the LORD, the God of Israel—he is the God who is in Jerusalem" (Ezra 1:2-3). This marked the end of the exile and the beginning of restoration.

Returns from Babylon

The first thing Cyrus did was collect the vessels plundered from the temple by Nebuchadnezzar and had them "released into the charge of Mithredath the treasurer, who counted them out to Sheshbazzar the prince of Judah" (Ezra 1:8). Sheshbazzar was the Babylonian name of a Jewish court official who was probably the son of Judah's exiled King Jehoiachin. Cyrus then named Sheshbazzar governor of Judah, who led a group of deportees back to the homeland and they "laid the foundations of the house of God in Jerusalem" (Ezra 5:16).

A few years later Zerubbabel was named to replace Sheshbazzar as governor of Judah and he led a second group of deportees back to Judah. When they arrived they "set out to build the altar of the God of Israel" (Ezra 3:2), but opposition to the rebuilding of the temple quickly grew. The Samaritans, the former inhabitants of the northern kingdom, offered to help but Zerubbabel told them "You shall have no part with us in building a house to our God; but we alone will build to the LORD, the God of Israel, as King Cyrus of Persia has commanded us. Then the people of the land discouraged the people of Judah, and made them afraid to build" (Ezra 4:3-4).

A Natural History of Scripture

Too much time passed by, so God raised up new prophets to exhort Zerubbabel to return to rebuilding the temple. The prophet Haggai said "Is it a time for you yourselves to live in your paneled houses, while this house lies in ruins?" (Haggai 1:4) and "Who is among you that saw this house in its former glory? How does it look to you now? Is it not in your sight as nothing?" (Haggai 2:3). The prophet Zechariah said "The hands of Zerubbabel have laid the foundation of this house; his hands shall also complete it" (Zechariah 4:9) and "Those who are far off shall come and help to build the temple of the LORD; and you shall know that the LORD of hosts has sent me to you. This will happen if you diligently obey the voice of the LORD your God" (Zechariah 6:15).

Construction of the Second Temple

King Darius of Persia finally discovered the old edict of King Cyrus, about letting the Jews rebuild their temple, and issued a political edict of his own: "I make a decree regarding what you shall do for these elders of the Jews for the rebuilding of this house of God: the cost is to be paid to these people, in full and without delay, from the royal revenue" (Ezra 6:8). Upon its completion, the people of Israel dedicated the second temple and returned to celebrating the commanded festivals. Their theological truths were restored because they again were the people of Israel living in their promised land. What was different was the lack of a monarchy, replaced by governors and high priests, and the slow demise of prophets,[31] replaced by inspired writings.

A Natural History of Scripture

The Poetic Writing of Job

The gradual transition from prophetic seers to poetic writers was a natural step. Harvard Professor James Kugel has made the observation that biblical prophets might have been like modern poets: "We do not know who the very first poet was, but after a while, there simply were poets, even inspired poets. Nobody asked, 'Who made you a poet?' People simply asked, 'What have you got to say?'"[32] The poetic story of Job had a lot to say.

Written after the experience of the exile, Job was the retelling of an ancient folk tale. One of the survivors "used this old legend to ask fundamental questions about the nature of God and his responsibility for the sufferings of humanity."[33] The wisdom of the time assured that divine justice would prevail, but the exile didn't feel like divine justice. The poetic work of Job expressed this contradiction with the explanation that patience was needed during confusing times, because divine wisdom was beyond our grasp. The best answer we got was "Truly the fear of the Lord, that is wisdom; and to depart from evil is understanding" (Job 28:28).

The Priestly Source

At this point in history, the sacred writings had been preserved, editing had begun, and a group of priests wrote yet another major source of material. This group wrote most of the book of Leviticus, along with a smattering of stories found throughout Genesis, Exodus, and Numbers. Their account of creation was deemed significant enough that later editors

A Natural History of Scripture

used it to begin the Hebrew Scriptures. The following is an accounting of how this alternative creation story might have come about, based on the background stories of its historical setting.

It had been a long and arduous journey back to the Holy Land. Crossing the desert left in its wake a toll of death and suffering for those who chose to return. The priests themselves probably broke down and cried when they arrived at the site of their destroyed temple in Jerusalem. Yet something stirred inside them to take a passionate stand and proclaim that they were still God's people.

They were laughed at and ridiculed while in Babylon. The gods of that far off land seemed to have won the battle against their God. Even some of the Israelites gave up on God and turned to worshipping the foreign gods. But these priests had something to say. They knew from firsthand experience that the God of the exodus was alive and well, and had just led them out of exile.

First of all, something had to be done about their beloved creation story (Genesis 2:4-25). It had been written some five hundred years earlier and no longer spoke of their experience. The God of that earlier story was a personal God who walked in the cool of the evening in the Garden of Eden. A new story was needed that would share a more complete picture of God: a tale that would show how small humans fit in the grandeur of the universe; and a religious truth that would balance the simple old story of God's relational character with a complex new story of God's ultimate power and control.

As thoughts began to form, a whole new threat from the ancient western world came to their attention. The Greek Empire was growing and the number-philosophy of

A Natural History of Scripture

Pythagoras was all the rage. To Pythagoras "the connection between shapes and numbers was deep and mystical. Every number-shape had a hidden meaning, and the most beautiful number-shapes were sacred."[34] Since the Pythagorean philosophy saw numbers and shapes as equivalent, it was obvious that zero didn't exist. How could a person make a shape out of nothing? So the Hebrew priests defiantly began their new story by writing that the earth was created from "a formless void" (Genesis 1:2). The entire Pythagorean universe could be understood through the mathematics of number-philosophy. Essentially mathematics was their god, and zero would terribly disrupt the neat Pythagorean universe. That's how the Hebrew priests toppled this lifeless idol: the simple introduction of the void. It was an innovative addition to the beginning of the creation story, but in a far more important way it drove a wedge between the Hebrew people and the Greek world.

It was not that the Hebrews wanted trouble, but their God-given land was still under foreign control and the least they could do was stake out the territory of their story and loudly proclaim false gods when and where they saw them. Greek philosophy was wrong. The priests wanted it known that the world was created and is governed not by the god of ratios, but by the one true God of the universe.

Enuma Elish and Gilgamesh

The rest of their new creation story would take on the plethora of creation myths of polytheism. The priests must have been appalled while in Babylon at the rampant worship of gods, so

A Natural History of Scripture

the attack they chose to use was the general outline of the Babylonian creation myth, *Enuma Elish* (*see below for an outlined comparison of the two stories*).[35] This can be verified because the original story was found on seven clay tablets in Nineveh in the mid-1800s. Remarkably similar to the Genesis creation account, the *Enuma Elish* moved from chaos to order and ended with the gods resting. The inescapable fact is that the *Enuma Elish* predated the Genesis story.

Archeologists also discovered the story of Gilgamesh[36] on twelve clay tablets in Nineveh around the same time as the discovery of the *Enuma Elish*. Our interest in this story concerns its relationship to the Hebrew Scriptures, because the eleventh tablet tells the story of a great flood. The hero in the Gilgamesh story is told to build a ship and include animals. After a great storm, a dove and a raven are sent out. The intrigue for us is the fact that not only does the Gilgamesh story sound strikingly like the biblical account of the flood (Genesis 6:19; 8:6-8), it also predates the Genesis story. If this is shocking, rest assured it was also shocking to church and synagogue. The traditional belief was that the creation and flood stories were literal history.

Genesis 1:1-2:3 and Enuma Elish

Genesis 1:1-2:3	Enuma Elish
1. The deep enveloped in Darkness.	1. Apsu and Tiamat enveloped in Darkness.
2. Creation of light.	2. Appearance of Marduk, "Sun of the Heavens."

A Natural History of Scripture

3. Creation of a dome called Sky.	3. Creation of sky from half of the body of Tiamat after battle with Marduk.
4. Creation of dry land by the gathering of waters.	4. Creation of dry land.
5. Creation of lights in the dome of the Sky.	5. Creation of constellations.
6. Creation of humankind to have dominion over all creation.	6. Creation of humankind to serve the gods.
7. God rests.	7. The gods rest.

Figure 2

We have now had 150 years to process this confusion and most scholars today see the stories of Genesis 1-11 as reactions against the polytheistic beliefs of the Babylonians. The priestly stories of creation and the flood were rewrites of original Babylonian stories, from the truth of monotheism. They were stories that embodied truth in the same way poems and parables embody truth.

The biblical creation and flood stories are not historical or literal truths. Far more importantly, the stories embody the theological truth that God is the creator of the universe. With the completion of their new creation story (Genesis 1:1-2:3), the priests had taken a stand against both East and West. In their isolated status, they shared a story that affirmed order out of chaos, victory out of defeat, and the truth of monotheism.

A Natural History of Scripture

Editing the Primary History

As new prophets successfully inspired belief in new creation and a new exodus, priests brought newness to the five existing Hebrew texts through editing. Genesis and Exodus were the result of editing together stories from: the Yahwist tradition; the Elohist revision; and their own Priestly Source. Leviticus and Numbers, written mostly by the priests, were attached to Genesis and Exodus, and the four books were joined to the Deuteronomic source. Genesis, Exodus, Leviticus, Numbers, and Deuteronomy became known as the Law, but their task was to enshrine the sacred story of God's people from creation to promised land.

The Deuteronomistic History became known as the Former Prophets, and their task was to continue the story where it left off in the books of the Law. Joshua, Judges, Samuel, and Kings told the story from promised land to exile. These nine books, composed of the Law and the Former Prophets, are called the Primary History because they tell the full story of Israel's beginnings.

Professor David Noel Freedman has uncovered the work of an even later editor in the internal structure of the Primary History.[37] Freedman suggests that the nine books from Genesis to Kings show a methodical breaking of the commandments, producing the final exile. Since the commandments were not delivered until the book of Exodus, the first two commandments were broken there. Exodus 20:3 prohibits apostasy and Exodus 20:4 prohibits idolatry, and the Hebrews manage to violate them both in Exodus 32:8, beginning their downward spiral.

A Natural History of Scripture

The third commandment prohibits blasphemy (Exodus 20:7) and it is broken in the third book (Leviticus 24:10-17). The fourth commandment concerns the Sabbath (Exodus 20:8). It is broken in the fourth book (Numbers 15:32-36) and is so utterly out of place in its current context that one becomes suspicious that a late editor is placing stories to make a point about breaking the Ten Commandments. The fifth commandment is about parenting (Exodus 20:12), disobeyed in the fifth book (Deuteronomy 21:18-21).

Commandments six through eight depart from the list in Exodus as this story unfolds. Rather than dealing in order with murder, adultery, and stealing, the Primary History follows the order of stealing, murder, and adultery. This order can be found in Jeremiah 7:9, hinting that our hidden editor may well have been Jeremiah's scribe Baruch. The alternate order of commandments six, seven, and eight in Jeremiah are violated in that order in the sixth, seventh, and eighth books of the Primary History.

The sixth commandment against stealing is violated in the sixth book (Joshua 7:11). The seventh commandment is against murder, which is the rare Hebrew word *ratsach*. This word and its violation appear in the seventh book (Judges 20:4-5). The eighth commandment prohibits adultery and is violated by King David in the eighth book (2 Samuel 11:2-4). The ninth commandment prohibits false witness (Exodus 20:16), and the infamous Jezebel breaks it (1 Kings 21:1-14). The tenth commandment prohibits coveting (Exodus 20:17), which concerns motivation rather than action. Adhering to the tenth commandment, Freedman concludes, eliminates the chance of breaking commandments six through nine.

A Natural History of Scripture

Canonizing the Primary History

The full process of canonizing the Hebrew books took about two thousand years. The oral stage gave way to the writing stage, which gave way to the prophetic stage, which gave way to the editing stage. Once the books of the Hebrew Bible made it to their final form, they still had to compete with many other scrolls as candidates for being deemed worthy as documents that shared the faith of the Hebrew people. This process is called canonization or the formation of the biblical canon. The Greek word *canon* means straight rod or standard. Each of these stages effected the formation of the Bible as we know it today.

Actually, the whole notion of biblical canon has undergone new thinking on how it eventually became accepted. The last quarter of the twentieth century saw the academic world work on developing a secular canon of non-biblical works. The interesting result was the opinion that literary works fight their way to canonicity through their "strangeness, a mode of originality that either cannot be assimilated, or that so assimilates us that we cease to see it as strange."[38]

A literary critic has agreed that "the canonicity of the Bible is by no means the simple and assured phenomenon of enshrining doctrine in text that it is often assumed to be."[39] He suggests that the development of a canon is most instructive at the boundary between acceptance and rejection and that the last books to make their way into the canon probably made it out of literary power and sheer popularity.

The first books to make their way into the Hebrew canon were the books of the Law and the books of the Former

A Natural History of Scripture

Prophets. The books of the Law (also known as the Torah or the Pentateuch) are Genesis, Exodus, Leviticus, Numbers, and Deuteronomy. The books of the Former Prophets are Joshua, Judges, 1 and 2 Samuel, and 1 and 2 Kings. This sequence of books "is clearly a story line beginning with creation and ending with the Babylonian destruction of Jerusalem and the exile."[40]

More Returns from Babylon

When Ezra led a third group of deportees back to Palestine, he brought with him a copy of Mosaic law. Even though the Law and the Former Prophets had both been canonized by the Hebrew people, it was obvious that the Law was rising in importance and prominence. The people of Israel gathered one day and "told the scribe Ezra to bring the book of the law of Moses, which the LORD had given to Israel" (Nehemiah 8:1).

Nehemiah heard that the people of Israel were in trouble, so he asked the King's permission to leave Babylon and visit Jerusalem. After inspection he announced "You see the trouble we are in, how Jerusalem lies in ruins with its gates burned. Come let us rebuild the wall of Jerusalem, so that we may no longer suffer disgrace" (Nehemiah 2:17). In spite of local objection, he completed the job in less than two months and had the wall dedicated (Nehemiah 6:15; 12:27). He also became governor of Israel and instituted religious reform.

A Natural History of Scripture

Postexilic Prophets

Obadiah

Now that the Jewish community was slowly being restored, it was time to vent some frustrations. Obadiah received a vision against Edom and said "For the slaughter and violence done to your brother Jacob, shame shall cover you, and you shall be cut off forever" (Obadiah 1:10). The father of the Edomites was Esau, who's twin brother Jacob was the father of the Israelites. The tension with this neighboring kingdom was the lack of help from kinfolk during the fall of Jerusalem. Obadiah's opinion was that the Edomite's lack of justice would gain them divine judgment.

Haggai

While Haggai's five sayings were uttered in 520 BC, they were not written down until the fifth century. Haggai exhorted Zerubbabel to complete the temple, with the encouragement that it would be greater than the first temple built by Solomon (Haggai 2:9). The purpose of the temple would be to have a sacred space where one could experience the divine presence. If they finish the task, the Lord said through Haggai, "from this day on I will bless you" (Haggai 2:19).

A Natural History of Scripture

Zechariah

Getting tired of prophets? Think about this for a moment: the biblical canon only enshrined the prophecies that came true. Chapters 1-8 of Zechariah were contemporary with Haggai during the Persian period, while chapters 9-14 spoke of the Greeks (Zechariah 9:13) and therefore must date to the Greek period. Zechariah shared eight visions, which began to develop the imagery of Jewish apocalyptic thought. He encouraged Zerubbabel to complete the restoration of the temple because it would not be "by might, nor by power, but by my spirit, says the LORD of hosts" (Zechariah 4:6).

Written by spiritual disciples of Zechariah, the second part elaborated on messianic expectations and apocalyptic themes. First envisioning the Greek overthrow of Persian power in Jerusalem, this prophet then shared the arrival of the messiah: "Lo, your king comes to you; triumphant and victorious is he, humble and riding on a donkey, on a colt, the foal of a donkey" (Zechariah 9:9). Feeling the need to be cleansed of sin, Jerusalemites would martyr their shepherd king and a remnant of his flock would be purified (Zechariah 13:7-9).

Joel

Using a locust plague on the country as a warning of God's judgment, Joel described this as the day of the LORD. First he exhorted his people to "rend your heart and not your clothing" (Joel 2:13), then "afterward I will pour out my spirit on all flesh; your sons and your daughters shall prophesy, your old men shall dream dreams, and your young men shall see visions" (Joel 2:28). If the people successfully repented, they could defend themselves from the surrounding nations (Joel 3:10) and the reward would be that "Judah shall be inhabited forever, and Jerusalem to all generations" (Joel 3:20).

Malachi

This prophet added to the concept of the day of the Lord by saying "See, I am sending my messenger to prepare the way before me, and the Lord whom you seek will suddenly come to his temple" (Malachi 3:1). Reestablishing the presence of God in the temple without the ark of the covenant would be an important and significant task for the restored community. Malachi then defined the messenger by saying "Lo, I will send you the prophet Elijah before the great and terrible day of the LORD comes" (Malachi 4:5).

After the recording of the prophet Malachi, "the age of the prophets comes to an end. From now on, Israel's leaders will have to rely on God's previously enunciated words, written in the Torah and in the writings of the prophets, in their efforts to decipher His will. Humankind is now on its own, with only the written records of God's will, not direct revelation, to guide it."[41]

Jonah

With the demise of prophecy and the advent of nationalism, an unknown author recorded on old popular

A Natural History of Scripture

legend and twisted it to reflect Israel's original mission to become a blessing to all (Malachi 4:5). The story was set in preexilic times where Jonah was called to preach repentance to Nineveh. Jonah did not like his call because he would rather prophesy about Nineveh's imminent destruction, so he sailed to the farthest point he could find.

Losing this disagreement with the LORD, "Jonah set out and went to Nineveh" (Jonah 3:3). To his great horror, the people of Nineveh repented and "God changed his mind about the calamity that he had said he would bring upon them" (Jonah 3:10). Jonah was so grieved that he begged God to kill him. God denied the request and instead taught him a lesson: "should I not be concerned about Nineveh, that great city, in which there are more than a hundred and twenty thousand persons who do not know their right hand from their left, and also many animals?" (Jonah 4:11). We get the lesson. Bigotry is never a part of God's ways.

Another Poetic Writing

The Psalms were a collection of one hundred and fifty poems[42] composed from Davidic times to postexilic times. These lyrical verses were finally written down for use in the temple of Zerubbabel, and were sung with dancing and music. Representing a wide variety of classifications, the Psalms were divided into five books.[43] This was done as an imitation of the Pentateuch, showing the great importance the Psalms had in the ritual and liturgy of the Jewish people.

A Natural History of Scripture

The Chronicler's History

At this time, another individual or group of people stepped forward and chronicled the history of the Jewish people. The existing Deuteronomistic History ended on a bad note, with the demise of the Davidic monarchy. The Chronicler's History was going to end on the good note of the restoration of the temple (2 Chronicles 36:23). This story ran from the creation of the world to the beginnings of the Persian Empire, paralleling the Genesis through Kings version.

The Chronicler was careful to cast the LORD in a better light, because the task was to walk the tight rope of sharing a glorious but failed past. For example, the older history shared that the LORD was angry with Israel, so he incited David to take a dreaded, tax-oriented census (2 Samuel 24:1). The Chronicler doesn't want a LORD who is angry, so the newer history shared that "Satan stood up against Israel, and incited David to count the people of Israel" (1 Chronicles 21:1).

The Chronicler also wanted to shed a better light on King David, so he neatly avoided the surreptitious story of David and Bathsheba. He also gave an assist to King Solomon, who had been reported to decline in spirituality in his later years, by reporting only the glorious deeds of Solomon. After telling about the divided monarchy, he took the evil King Manasseh and added a detail unknown in the Deuteronomistic History; he said that Manasseh repented (2 Chronicles 33:10-13). Originally one scroll, like Samuel and Kings, Chronicles was later divided into two.

Many scholars believe that the author of Chronicles was also the author of Ezra and Nehemiah, and that Ezra and

A Natural History of Scripture

Nehemiah were originally written as supplements to the book of Chronicles. This matter is disputed and "some recent scholars have strongly urged that Ezra and Nehemiah be treated as independent works."[44] The Chronicler's History would not make its way into scripture until the Writings section of the Hebrew Scriptures was canonized. Ezra and Nehemiah would be put before 1 and 2 Chronicles, which would ultimately form the concluding four books of the Hebrew Scriptures.

The Fall of Palestine to the Greeks

After the Chronicler's History, the biblical record is obscure. Even the arrival of Alexander the Great is nowhere found in the Bible. Considering Jewish life during Persian domination worked out pretty well, the fall of Palestine to the Greeks was probably not welcomed. Alexander conquered a vast area including Egypt, Greece, Asia Minor, Persia, and Babylon. Now that God's people were living in many different places, a need to translate the Hebrew Scriptures into other languages grew. This was not preferable, because translation always involves interpretation, which is where we now turn.

A Natural History of Scripture

Chapter 5
Translators: Diversity Strikes Again

Prenatal Stage: Storytellers	Infant Stage: Writers		Adolescent Stage: Editors			Adult Stage: Standardizers	
Oral History	Written History	Pro-phets	Priests	**Trans-lators**	Evan-gelists	Politi-cians	Pub-lishers
2000 BC	950 BC	750 BC	586 BC	332 BC	63 BC	AD 144	AD 1454	NOW

Whoever translates a verse in the Bible literally has perpetrated a fraud, and whoever interpolates his own addition to it has perpetrated blasphemy (Qiddushin, 49a).

Unfortunately, when the biblical stories were written down, they were recorded on perishable material. With use and time, the texts wore out and had to be recopied. This was done many times over the centuries by a group of people called scribes. Language and culture changed over time, thereby causing difficulties in deciding what words to use in each new generation. We see this problem alive today in the explosion of new translations. As the Bible was

A Natural History of Scripture

growing in complexity, it experienced more diversity, which is a natural consequence of evolution.

More Trouble with Words

In biblical times, successive waves of conquerors (the Babylonians, Persians, Greeks, Egyptians, Syrians, and then Romans) introduced new words and ideas into the Hebrew language. Scribes not only recopied the stories, they had to be interpreters to perform their task. They also had to speak to each new generation with current words. The problem was that the new words did not always properly express what the original meant.

Now this is important:
translations are always interpretations.

The team of translators who decide what English word to use in modern versions base their decisions on their theology. This is not a bad thing, but it is extremely useful to be aware of the theological commitment of the team of translators for your favorite version. At critical points, teams will often translate based on their theology rather than using the best English word that most closely expresses the original Hebrew. I relentlessly teach this concept when leading Bible studies and keep constant watch for this hidden problem, because translators often seek to share their theology rather than God's Word. My belief is that when we are honest with the text, the text will be honest with us.

A Natural History of Scripture

A Difficult Answer

The only way to avoid this hidden problem is to learn biblical Hebrew, but this still does not solve the problem because the Hebrew writing system itself complicates the task of translation. Only consonants were written down (no vowels) and biblical Hebrew contained no punctuation and no space between letters. Here's an English sentence for you to experience the difficulty of translating Hebrew: FLLNWHR. Take a moment and try inserting vowels and spaces. What ways could this sentence read? Should it start with a vowel or the consonant that is present? Is it a question or a statement? Some ways it could be read are "I fall nowhere," "If all now here," or even "Fallen whore." Interpretation again is important, and the way this obstacle was overcome was by translating the sentence in its context. You would have to know what was being said before and after the sentence to get the best translation, which is also the best way to understand the Bible in any language today.

The difficulty of this task was historically honored by having the position of scribe become one of great authority. These ancient biblical interpreters appear to have followed a common set of assumptions when translating the biblical text: 1) the Bible is a cryptic document full of hidden meaning, 2) Scripture constitutes one great Book of Instruction, and as such is a fundamentally relevant text, 3) Scripture is perfect and perfectly harmonious, so mistakes (Genesis 15:3 asserts that the Israelites "will be oppressed for 400 years" in Egypt, while Exodus 12:41 speaks of 430 years) simply need clarified by proper interpretation, and 4) all of Scripture is divinely inspired.[45]

A Natural History of Scripture

The Official Language

Greek rapidly became the official language as Hellenism spread over the Near East with major centers in Alexandria and Antioch. When Alexander died in 323 BC, it turned out that he was irreplaceable. The next two decades saw many would-be successors battle for power, and the split of the empire. Eventually, a man named Ptolemy gained control of Egypt and ruled from Alexandria, while a man named Seleucus gained control of Syria and ruled from Antioch. Palestine was controlled by the Ptolemies until 198 BC, then by the Seleucids until 175 BC. The Maccabean revolt brought independent rule back to the Jews for a little over a century, until the Romans conquered them in 63 BC.

Ptolemaic Rule

The Ptolemaic rulers "permitted the Jewish Council of Elders, which had apparently existed since the time of Ezra, to continue to administer the country, under the chairmanship of the high priest."[46] This administration had no political independence, and the chief priest collected and paid taxes to the Ptolemies on behalf of the people. While many Jews chose to move to Alexandria for economic reasons, others were deported there by Ptolemy I. Ptolemy II freed the deportees and Alexandria's Jewish population quickly became the largest of the postexilic era.

A Natural History of Scripture

Another Poetic Writing

The book of Proverbs was a compilation of about 375 sayings of Israel's historically wise ones. Some of the collection was preexilic while other parts of it were postexilic. These proverbial statements are poetic expressions of wisdom learned by experience and applied to the pursuit of a successful life. They provided practical guidelines that often were more human than divine (i.e., Proverbs 23:13). With the demise of prophecy, the book of Proverbs was finally written down because it was recognized as a major source of wisdom.

The Megillot

The week I was writing this section of the book, I just happened to also be teaching the Megillot for an adult Bible study. The class was intrigued that several of these books had trouble getting into the final canon of Hebrew scripture. They even began to wonder why they made it at all. This is a wonderfully healthy approach to scripture. The fact that we study the Bible shows our belief that it is the Word of God. The fact that we can raise fundamental questions about it shows an understanding that it is not God's words. It is a very human product that defines our lives as believers in the one God.

Megillot is the Hebrew word for five scrolls, imitating the five books of the Law as does the five books of the Psalms. Between the fourth and second centuries BC, these particular writings were recorded and gained importance by being read at the following Jewish holidays: The Song of Solomon at the Passover Feast, Ruth at Pentecost (the holiday celebrating the giving of Torah to Moses on Mount Sinai), Lamentations at the 9th of Av (the date on which the temple was destroyed), Ecclesiates at the Feast of Tabernacles, and Esther at the Feast of Purim.

The Song of Solomon

Although this collection of love poems mentions King Solomon as its author (Song of Solomon 1:1), his name only appears in the third person. The book's style and themes put the work to a far later time than Solomon's, perhaps the third or second century BC. At surface level, the Song is a celebration of human sexuality. At a deeper level, it is a celebration of the love between God and God's people. At any level, it complemented the quite different language of law and prophecy.

My class read this book as a play, featuring a bride, bridegroom, and chorus. The beauty of the love poetry inspired them, but the question still arose as to what made it worthy of inclusion in the Bible. The answer must lie in the purpose of the song, and that has never been agreed upon. Is it a collection of love poems, a Judean wedding song, a celebration of the seasons, a drama, or a symbolic story? That's what makes it fun. We can read it from many different angles and still get something out of it.

Ruth

A Natural History of Scripture

This short story was like Jonah and Isaiah 40-55, in that it confirmed the LORD was concerned for people of every nation. It helped counter the opinion in Judaism that said marriage to foreigners was wrong, which was the stance of Ezra and Nehemiah. The plot focused on Naomi, an Israelite, and her Moabite daughter-in-law, Ruth. The foreigner made a wonderful commitment to her mother-in-law: "Where you go, I will go; where you lodge, I will lodge; your people shall be my people, and your God my God" (Ruth 1:16).

Although the story focuses on human action rather than divine intervention, it is clear that the covenant community is called to enlarge and include Gentiles who show faith in God. This can be seen in the response to Ruth from one of Naomi's relatives: "All that you have done for your mother-in-law since the death of your husband has been fully told me, and how you left your father and mother and your native land and came to a people that you did not know before. May the LORD reward you for your deeds, and may you have a full reward from the LORD, the God of Israel, under whose wings you have come for refuge!" (Ruth 2:11-12). The final editor of the story drove home the point in an unforgettable way by having the Jew Boaz and the Moabitess Ruth become the great grandparents of King David (Ruth 4:18-22).

Lamentations

This scroll is a collection of five poetic laments written after the fall of Jerusalem to express the grief and despair of the people. As the Megillot slowly brought liturgical life

A Natural History of Scripture

centuries later to annual feasts and fasts, this work gave voice to the reason for the disaster: "The LORD gave full vent to his wrath; he poured out his hot anger, and kindled a fire in Zion that consumed its foundations" (Lamentations 4:11). Yet even in the midst of judgment, this book offered the balance of promise: "The steadfast love of the LORD never ceases, his mercies never come to an end" (Lamentations 3:22). One of the beauties of this book is that it gives permission to vent anger, even at God. In other words, there is nothing that we cannot bring to divine attention.

Ecclesiastes

We are told that the author of this book is "the Teacher, the son of David, king in Jerusalem" (Ecclesiastes 1:1), traditionally thought to be King Solomon, but words from a much later time period are used. The Hebrew word for teacher is *Qoheleth*, who was also described as wise (Ecclesiastes 12:9). *Qoheleth* was probably an important official in third century Jerusalem who expressed the views of an elite group of people. He or she (*Qoheleth* is the feminine form of the word) counseled listeners to accept the current economic and social conditions, because opposition was useless: "Keep the king's command because of your sacred oath. Do not be terrified; go from his presence, do not delay when the matter is unpleasant, for he does whatever he pleases. For the word of the king is powerful, and who can say to him, 'What are you doing?'" (Ecclesiastes 8:2-4).

A Natural History of Scripture

Since the teacher taught that "all is vanity and a chasing after wind" (Ecclesiastes 1:14), the ultimate advice was "There is nothing better for mortals than to eat and drink, and find enjoyment in their toil" (Ecclesiastes 2:24). These brief comments from *Qoheleth* "indicate the background to an opposition between the aristocracy in Judaea (or at least part of them) on the one hand and the ordinary people on the other, which steadily increased over the course of time. This opposition was finally to lead, among other things, to armed conflict in the time of the Maccabees."[47]

Esther

This scroll is a Jewish novel, which addresses the question of how a Jew should live in society. The tale probably originated among the Babylonians because "Esther is the Aramaic name of the Babylonian goddess Ishtar, and Mordecai—whose legend may at one time have been separate—means 'worshipper of Marduk', the Babylonian god."[48] This is often found to be shocking, because many people have never heard it taught as anything other than history.

The story was transposed into a Jewish novel to speak to the dispersed Jews living in a Gentile world. It reflected nationalistic pride when antagonism toward Gentiles ran high among Jews, shortly prior to the Maccabean revolt. It also purported to give the 'historical' basis for the Festival of Purim: "These days should be remembered and kept throughout every generation, in every family, province, and city; and these days of Purim should never fall into disuse among the Jews,

A Natural History of Scripture

nor should the commemoration of these days cease among their descendants" (Esther 9:28).

The Greek Translation of Hebrew Texts

During the reign of King Ptolemy II, an Egyptian high priest published a history of Egypt in which he contradicted the Hebrew account of the exodus. With racial prejudice swelling, the Jews of Alexandria countered with a Greek translation of the Hebrew Scriptures. This language was now replacing Aramaic throughout most of the Near East and the Greek Bible came to be known as the Septuagint, meaning seventy. This is because it was supposedly the work of seventy translators, working under divine inspiration.

These Greek translators used a literal Hebrew-to-Greek method rather than a freer one. While this development enhanced understandings between Jews and Greeks, it unfortunately represented the current demise of the Hebrew language. The Septuagint also served the purpose of extending history into the Greek-Roman Period. The importance of this work is that it gives us ideas on how we got our Bible.

The Egyptian Jews located the story of Ruth between Judges and 1 Samuel. This tells us that they accepted Ruth as canonical. In fact, they also accepted: 1) the rest of the Megillot, 2) the books that came to be known as the Latter Prophets, and 3) several others books that did not survive the final canonization process. *Figure 3 shows the books as they are ordered in most existing copies of the Septuagint.*

A Natural History of Scripture

The Septuagint

Genesis	Esther	Hosea
Exodus	Judith	Amos
Leviticus	Tobit	Micah
Numbers	1 Maccabees	Joel
Deuteronomy	2 Maccabees	Obadiah
Joshua	3 Maccabees	Jonah
Judges	4 Maccabees	Nahum
Ruth	Psalms	Habakkuk
1 Samuel	Proverbs	Zephaniah
2 Samuel	Ecclesiastes	Haggai
1 Kings	Song of Solomon	Zechariah
2 Kings	Job	Malachi
1 Chronicles	Wisdom	Isaiah
2 Chronicles	Sirach	Baruch
1 Esdras (Ezra and Nehemiah)	Psalms of Solomon	Song of the three Jews
Letter of Jeremiah	Susanna	Bel and the Dragon
Ezekiel	Daniel	

Figure 3

The Pseudepigrapha

The term pseudepigrapha literally means false writings. It comes from a Greek word, which more specifically means writings with false authorship. These were writings rejected by the Jews and later by the Christians. There are 65 documents

A Natural History of Scripture

that have received the traditional collective title of Pseudepigrapha, broken into four categories.

Apocalyptic Literature

Apocalyptic comes from a Greek word that means revelation or disclosure. It is used to describe both a type of literature and a preoccupation with end of time scenarios. Unfortunately "there is presently no consensus regarding the precise definition of this adjective."[49] The Bible contains many apocalyptic sections,[50] while the Hebrew Scriptures accepted the book of Daniel and the Christian Sequel accepted the book of Revelation as full representatives of this kind of material.

Testaments

This type of material shared the last words and wills of model figures. Common features included instructions on righteousness, utterances of blessings and curses, descriptions of apocalypses, and exhortations to avoid certain temptations. An example of this type of material can be found in Genesis 49.

Legends

This group of writings often featured expansions of biblical material, explanations of the superiority of Judaism, apologetics, missionary purpose, celebrations of God's

A Natural History of Scripture

covenant, and God's guidance of the faithful. Originally told as oral legends, some of the stories evolved into the documents collected in the Pseudepigrapha.

Miscellaneous

This section included wisdom literature (similar to Job, Proverbs, and Ecclesiastes), philosophical literature, prayers (similar to Matt 6:9b-13), psalms, odes, and fragments of lost Judeo-Hellenistic works.

*See Figure 4
on the next two pages
for a listing of of the 65 documents.*

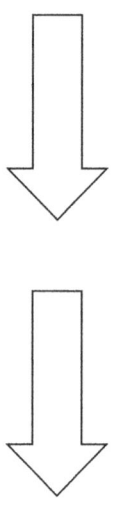

A Natural History of Scripture

The Pseudepigrapha

Apocalyptic Literature

1 Enoch
2 Enoch
3 Enoch
Sibylline Oracles
Treatise of Shem
Apocryphon of Ezekiel
Apocalypse of Zephaniah
4 Ezra
Apocalypse of Ezra
Vision of Ezra
Questions of Ezra
Revelation of Ezra
Apocalypse of Sedrach
2 Baruch
3 Baruch
Apocalypse of Abraham
Apocalypse of Adam
Apocalypse of Elijah
Apocalypse of Daniel

Testaments

Testaments of the Twelve Patriarchs
Testament of Job
Testaments of the Three Patriarchs
Testament of Moses
Testament of Solomon
Testament of Adam

Legends

Letter of Aristeas
Jubilees
Martyrdom and Ascension of Isaiah
Joseph and Aseneth
Life of Adam and Eve
Pseudo-Philo
The Lives of the Prophets
Ladder of Jacob
4 Baruch
Jannes and Jambres
History of the Rechabites
Eldad and Modad
History of Joseph

Miscellaneous

Ahiqar
3 Maccabees
4 Maccabees

A Natural History of Scripture

Pseudo-Phocylides	Theodotus
The Sentences of the Syriac Menander	Orphica
	Ezekiel the Tragedian
More Psalms of David	Pseudo-Greek Poets
Prayer of Manasseh	Aristobulus
Psalms of Solomon	Demetrius the Chronographer
Hellenistic Synagogal Prayers	
	Aristeas the Exegete
Prayer of Joseph	Eupolemus
Prayer of Jacob	Psuedo-Eupolemus
Odes of Solomon	Cleodomus Malcus
Philo the Epic Poet	Artapanus
	Pseudo-Hecatae[51]

Figure 4

The Aramaic Translation of Hebrew Texts

While the Jews in Egypt had adopted Greek as their tongue and translated the biblical writings into the Septuagint, the Jews in Palestine and Mesopotamia adopted Aramaic as their tongue and translated the biblical writings into what are known as the Targumim, plural for Targum. The Aramaic translation of the Pentateuch is believed to have originated in Palestine by a man named Onqelos and the Aramaic translation of the Prophets is believed to have originated in Palestine by a man named Jonathan.

There is no official collection of Targumim for the remaining writings, but Aramaic translations exist for Job,

A Natural History of Scripture

Psalms, Proverbs, Lamentations, Canticles (Song of Solomon), Ruth, Qoheleth (Ecclesiastes), Esther, and Chronicles. Fragments of Targumim were also discovered at Qumran. The Aramaic translations were much freer than the Greek, and often moved more into the field of interpretation rather than translation.

Let's pause for a moment and consider Guided Exercise #5 on the next page.

Seleucid Rule

After more than a century of battles, the Seleucid monarch Antiochus III beat the Egyptian forces at the headwaters of the Jordan to take over the rule of Palestine. It was about this time that a new power was appearing on the political scene. The Romans had recently defeated Hannibal and now were in the midst of defeating the troops of Antiochus III, which is recorded in scripture (Daniel 11:18). As part of a peace agreement with Rome, Antiochus III let his second son, later to become Antiochus IV Epiphanes, go to Rome as a hostage.

After the assassination of Antiochus III, Seleucus IV brought a worsening relationship with the Jews. Antiochus IV was his successor and he interfered with Jewish religious affairs. He forced his way on the Jewish people by sending one of his generals to Palestine to enforce loyalty. Jersusalem was looted, Torahs were burned, and innocent people were killed. An altar to Zeus was erected in the temple and sacrifices to Greek gods were demanded from the Jews.

A Natural History of Scripture

Guided Exercise #5

Just as people sometimes use a foreign word in the midst of their work, like *caveat emptor* (Latin for buyer beware), the Hebrew Scriptures also have portions of Aramaic. Look up the following examples, which contain all of the Aramaic sections in the Hebrew Scriptures.

1. *Daniel 2:4b-7:28.* This is the longest sustained piece of Aramaic in the Hebrew Scriptures. Notice the footnote in the NRSV explains that the original is in Aramaic. Also note that the passage itself is introduced as being in Aramaic.

2. *Ezra 4:8-6:18, 7:12-26.* The first passage from Ezra was a letter written in Aramaic and included in this part of the book of Ezra. Notice that the footnote in the NRSV explains the passage continues through 6:18. The second passage from Ezra is a copy of a letter originally written in Aramaic. The fact that this letter is in Aramaic is listed in the NRSV annotation at the bottom of the page.

3. *Jeremiah 10:11.* This verse is the only Aramaic in the entire book of Jeremiah. The NRSV footnote mentions that the verse is in Aramaic.

4. *Genesis 31:47a (two words).* Footnote *d* in the NRSV explains the meaning of the original Aramaic words.

A Natural History of Scripture

The Maccabean Revolt

A priest named Mattathias was the first to refuse to offer a pagan sacrifice, and then he killed a fellow Jew who complied. To escape official retaliation, he hid among the hills and was joined by a number of Jews who were supportive. After his death in 166 BC, he was succeeded by his son Judas Maccabeus, who recaptured Jerusalem and reconsecrated the temple in 164 BC. This event is still commemorated annually at the Festival of the Dedication, which is more popularly known as Hanukkah. Mattathias' family is variously remembered as the Hasmoneans or the Maccabees, and their successful revolt for Jewish independence lasted the better part of a century.

Apocalyptic Literature

Apocalypse means disclosure, unveiling, or revelation. Apocalypses come from times of "national or community tribulation, and are not actual history, but, through symbols and signs, are interpretations of current history with its background and predictions of a future where tribulations and sorrows will give place to triumph and peace."[52] Apocalypticsm is also characterized by dualism, where there are two opposing personified forces, one good and the other evil, and by two distinct ages, the present age and the age to come.

It was during the Maccabean revolt that the book of Daniel was written down. To encourage his fellow sufferers, the author told six stories, set in earlier days in Babylon, to show how God helped faithful Jews triumph over their enemies. Then in four visions he interpreted current history

A Natural History of Scripture

and predicted the coming consummation of final Jewish victory.

The story section of the book told how Daniel was deported from Judah to Babylon. His friends refused to worship a golden idol; were thrown into a fiery furnace; then rescued by God (Daniel 3:1-30). Daniel himself was then thrown into a lion's den, but received divine protection (Daniel 6:1-28). The vision section of the book said that a son of man would come in the clouds and God would give him universal kingly power (Daniel 7:13-14). The author later identified the savior as the archangel Michael and provided the first clear reference to resurrection in the Hebrew Scriptures (Daniel 12:1-2).

Factions within Judaism

With newfound independence, the Jewish community was able to put its energy back into observance of the Torah. The passage of time caused the Torah to need updated, to keep it useful, so an oral tradition slowly developed to clarify the old laws. The status of this oral tradition produced three major factions within Judaism:

1) the Pharisees

2) the Sadduccees

3) the Essenes

A Natural History of Scripture

The Pharisees

The Hebrew word underlying *Pharisees* probably means "to separate." This group accepted the oral law as holy, traced its origin to Moses, and considered obedience to it morally mandatory. Their influence on Judaism was extensive and one of their major beliefs was that the kingdom of God would come when the people of God kept the law.

The Sadduccees

The Hebrew word underlying *Sadduccees* was probably Zadok, who was King David's High Priest. After the end of the monarchy, the office of High Priest assumed even greater importance. This didn't change until the period of Seleucid Rule, which was vigorously reclaimed by the Sadduccees after the Maccabean Revolt. The Sadduccees rejected the oral law of the Pharisees and such theological innovations as resurrection.

The Essenes and The Dead Sea Scrolls

In the spring of 1947, a young Bedouin shepherd found seven ancient Hebrew and Aramaic scrolls in a cave near the ruins called Khirbet Qumran by the Dead Sea (written between about 150 BC and 68 AD). The next nine years yielded the discovery of ten more caves containing a dozen scrolls and thousands of fragments. After tremendous political struggle, the scroll texts were finally released to scholars in 1991.

A Natural History of Scripture

Like the early Christians, the Essenes of Qumran "considered themselves to be the Israel of the end of days."[53] This comparison may help to explain the following discovery: 'the Way' is a self-designation of the early Christians, which is found only in Acts[54] among New Testament writings. However, the same use of 'the Way' occurs in "the Qumran writings to designate the mode of life of the Essenes."[55] *See the next few pages for a categorical listing of the books of the Dead Sea Scrolls.*[56]

The Dead Sea Scrolls

The Rules

The Community Rule
The Damascus Document
The Messianic Rule
The War Scroll
The Rule of War

The Temple Scroll

Some Observations of the Law
The Wicked and the Holy
Purities
Exhortation by the Master addressed to the Sons of Dawn
Register of Rebukes
Remonstrances

A Natural History of Scripture

Hymns and Poems

The Thanksgiving Hymns
Apocryphal Psalms
Non-canonical Psalms
Lamentations

Songs for the Holocaust of the Sabbath

Poetic Fragments on Jerusalem and King Jonathan

Calendars/Liturgies/Prayers

Calendars of Priestly Courses
Calendric Signs
Horoscopes
Phases of the Moon
A Zodiacal Calendar
Order of Divine Office
The Words of the Heavenly Lights
Liturgical Prayer
Prayers for Festivals
Daily Prayers
Hymn Celebrating the Morning and the Evening
Blessings
Benedictions
Confession Ritual
Purification Ritual
A Liturgical Work

A Natural History of Scripture

Apocalyptic Works

Apocryphal Weeks
Conquest of Egypt and Jerusalem
The Triumph of Righteousness
A Messianic Apocalypse

Wisdom Literature

The Seductress
Exhortation to Seek Wisdom
Parable of the Tree
A Sapiential Work
Bless, My Soul
Songs of the Sage
Beatitudes

Bible Interpretation

This group consists of:
Biblical Interpretations
Commentaries
Translations

Biblically-Based Apocryphal Works

This group consists of:
Testaments

A Natural History of Scripture

Apocryphons
Apocryphal Works

Miscellanea

The Copper Scroll
List of False Prophets
List of Netinim
Entry into the Covenant
Four Classes of the Community
The Two Ways
Hymnic Fragments
Two Qumran Ostraca

Figure 5

Canonization of the Latter Prophets

Many texts were circulating at this time, so the Jewish community needed to affirm which ones properly related the story of their relationship with God. The already canonized Law and Former Prophets told a complete story from creation to exile and also made four points: 1) it was not God who let us down in defeat, 2) it was us who let God down in disobedience, 3) it was God who sent prophets to tell us the way it is, and 4) if we take to heart that God meant what Moses and the prophets had been saying, then God would restore them.[57]

A Natural History of Scripture

These four points are also presented in the 15 case histories that became canonized as the Latter Prophets. These points were often stressed in the general themes of risings and fallings (i.e., Jeremiah 1:10) and the fourth point of restoration was commonly used for the ending. Based on length, these scrolls were known as the Major Prophets (Isaiah, Jeremiah, Ezekiel) and the Minor Prophets (Hosea, Joel, Amos, Obadiah, Jonah, Micah, Nahum, Habbakuk, Zephaniah, Haggai, Zechariah, and Malachi).

The designation of Latter Prophets simply specifies that they were ultimately placed after the Former Prophets in the canonical order of the Hebrew Scriptures. The further breakdown of Major Prophets and Minor Prophets simply refer to their size. The Major Prophets were each contained on a separate scroll, while the Minor Prophets were short enough to be recorded together on a single scroll. The Minor Prophets are also known as The Book of the Twelve. *Figure 6 shows the Latter Prophets in their proper historical context.*

The Fall of Palestine to the Romans

This period of time experienced an increase in domination by Rome under the leadership of General Pompey. In 64 BC the Seleucid realm became a new province of the Roman Empire, which then turned its attention to Judea as a buffer against the hostile rulers of Mesopotamia. Strife within the Hasmonean family made things easier for Rome because both Aristobulus II and his older brother Hyrcanus II wanted the throne and priesthood.

A Natural History of Scripture

The quarreling Hasmonean rulers lost no time in appealing to Pompey, who in turn seized Jerusalem, slaughtered many of its inhabitants, and did the unthinkable by stepping inside the holy of holies. The fall of Palestine to the Romans marked the end of Jewish independence, which would not be regained until AD 1948. Canonization of the Writings and the closing of the Hebrew canon would wait until after the destruction of the second temple. That would also be the time the Christian Sequel would begin coming together in earnest.

The Latter Prophets

The Major Prophets

NAME	PREEXILIC, EXILIC, OR POSTEXILIC	DATE
Isaiah	Preexilic (chapters 1-39)	742 BC
	Exilic (chapters 40-55)	540 BC
	Postexilic (chapters 56-66)	5th Century BC
Jeremiah	Preexilic	626 BC
Ezekiel	Preexilic (chapters 1-32)	590 BC
	Exilic (chapters 33-58)	585 BC

A Natural History of Scripture

The Minor Prophets

NAME	PREEXILIC, EXILIC, OR POSTEXILIC	DATE
Hosea	Preexilic	745 BC
Joel	Postexilic	5th Century BC
Amos	Preexilic	750 BC
Obadiah	Postexilic	5th Century BC
Jonah	Postexilic	5th Century BC
Micah	Preexilic	730 BC
Nahum	Preexilic	612 BC
Habakkuk	Preexilic	615 BC
Zephaniah	Preexilic	635 BC
Haggai	Postexilic	5th Century BC
Zechariah	Postexilic	5th Century BC
Malachi	Postexilic	5th Century BC

Figure 6

A Natural History of Scripture

Chapter 6
Evangelists: Adaptation at Work

Prenatal Stage: Storytellers	Infant Stage: Writers		Adolescent Stage: Editors			Adult Stage: Standardizers	
Oral History	Written History	Pro-phets	Priests	Trans-lators	Evan-gelists	Politi-cians	Pub-lishers
2000 BC	950 BC	750 BC	586 BC	332 BC	63 BC	AD 144	AD 1454 NOW

The Messiah was to be the great and powerful leader who delivered Israel from its oppressive overlords.[58]

Standing on top of the natural fortress of Masada is one of the world's oldest synagogues. The need for this kind of building probably came from the exile, when the Jewish people found themselves without land or temple. We can see the early origins of a worshipping community outside of Palestine in Ezekiel's prophecy: "Though I removed them far away among the nations, and though I scattered them among the countries, yet I have been a sanctuary to them for

A Natural History of Scripture

a little while in the countries where they have gone" (Ezekiel 11:16).

In their earliest forms, synagogues were simply gatherings of Jewish people for worship, study, and prayer. These meetings were probably held in private homes before the exile, and in public buildings after the exile. Synagogues served as temple-alternatives after the destruction of the temple, but they continued to grow in numbers even after Zerubbabel oversaw the building of the second temple. This was important because it let the Jewish faith continue outside the Holy Land and it set the stage for disagreements with the temple priests inside the Holy Land.

This was a unique time in history because an inventive spirit proliferated in the late Second Temple period. Even though the Law and the Prophets had been canonized, there was openness to alternative understandings of Torah and temple. Many of these works would eventually get censored in the canonization process, but they reveal a willingness to rewrite canonized scripture. The book of Jubilees did nothing less than correct a problem inherent in the Law. The question of Moses' authorship of the Law was swirling among the thinkers of the day, so this book resolved the problem. It had Moses go up the mountain for forty days where God said "Set your mind on everything which I shall tell you on this mountain, and write it in a book" (Jubilees 1:5).

Going even further, one of the Dead Sea Scrolls literally offered a replacement of Torah. This was done by having the voice of Yahweh recorded directly in the text without Moses serving as an intermediary. Instead of Moses saying what the Lord told him, the Temple Scroll offered direct, divine

A Natural History of Scripture

revelations like "I, YHWH, abide amongst the children of Israel for ever and ever" (Temple Scroll, column XLV, line 14). This served the purpose of creating a superior text. Other texts of this time began offering new theologies concerning such themes as Messiah and resurrection. It is into this volatile mix we now step as we continue the story of biblical composition.

Beginnings of the Christian Sequel

The theory of evolution says that gradualism produces variation, which must produce adaptation as a primary outcome. Adaptation is the localized result of a changing environment, and it is the central phenomenon of evolution. Massive unrest at the time of Jesus was destined to create an adaptation of Law. The creative force of evolution was ready to produce change, and the resulting story was the Gospel.

After Judea fell to the hands of the Romans, Hyrcanus was retained as high priest. He was allowed to govern Jewish affairs throughout the Dispersion, and this is where Julius Caesar also ordered religious freedom. The Romans eventually sent Herod to be king over Judea, thereby bringing an end to the Hasmonean dynasty. Herod then ordered the Jews to swear an oath of allegiance to Caesar and himself, but orthodox Jews objected and began talking of a messianic king. Herod considered this kind of talk an act of high treason and had people of questionable loyalty executed. While Herod managed to have the second temple rebuilt during his reign (37 BC—4 BC), his life ended in failing physical and mental health.

A Natural History of Scripture

The Romans never found things to come easy as they governed Palestine. In an attempt to raise higher taxes, a census was ordered, but this was met with the formation of a resistance group called the Zealots. Meanwhile, the Roman governor Pontius Pilate (AD 26—AD 36) retained Caiaphas as high priest, but he proved to be insensitive to the Jews. This was part of the social, political and religious climate in Judea at the time of Jesus. This scene served as the gestation time for the Christian Sequel which went through the same oral, writing, and editing, stages as the Hebrew scriptures. The main difference was the canonization time for the Christian Sequel was much shorter.

Jesus and the Silent Years

One problem we have with trying to reconstruct the historical life of Jesus is the precious little information to be found about him outside the Gospels. Biblical scholar Paula Fredricksen even goes so far as to suggest that the "single most solid fact about Jesus' life is his death."[59] Various opinions have been offered about his identity, none of which are conclusive. We are not certain about his social class, his cultural environment, or his religious orientation. Was he a Jewish reformer, a messiah of the apocalypse, a Greek-inclined sage, a Pharisaic interpreter of Torah, a revolutionary preacher, or a religious ascetic?

Some other thoughts about Jesus might be useful as we begin exploring the origin and formation of the Christian Sequel:

A Natural History of Scripture

- Jesus was raised as a Jew in Nazareth, geographically associating him with the Israelites of old rather than the Judahites.
- Jesus lived as a Jew in Capernaum, where his ministry focused on Jews (Matthew 15:24).
- Jesus died as a Jew in Jerusalem, where he was crucified after a Jewish trial found him to be a false Messiah (Mark 14:61-64) and a Roman trial found him to be a false King (Mark 15:12-15).

Also, Jesus never spoke to the Church, because it was not founded until after he died. He never wrote, but later disciples recorded his sayings. And little is known about what happened in the silent years immediately after the crucifixion of Jesus. What we do know is that somehow two strands of belief survived the destruction of the second temple. Of all the multiple Judaisms being practiced in the late Second Temple period, Christianity and rabbinic Judaism eventually emerged. Through radical changes, they separately solidified from a common Judahite heritage.

After the resurrection of Jesus and the arrival of Pentecost, the early church got started. Peter, James, and John emerged as the leaders of this new group of messianic Jews in Jerusalem because they were eyewitnesses of the Jesus event. Messianic Judaism was for Jews who believed Jesus was the Messiah, but then things got complicated when Gentiles started believing Jesus was the Messiah. Peter seemed willing to accept Gentiles, as long as they kept Mosaic law, but this was unacceptable to a man named Paul. These people faced an identity crisis and it should be noted that the name Christian was still in the future (Acts 11:26).

A Natural History of Scripture

Who were these people? Did conversion to messianic Judaism depend on faith or works? When Gentiles converted to messianic Judaism, did they have to begin following the Torah? When Jews converted to messianic Judaism, could they stop following the Torah? These sticky questions were not easy to answer, but after a conference in Jerusalem in AD 49, Peter agreed to evangelize the Jews while Paul gave his missionary energy to the Gentiles (Galatians 2:7-9).

Peter's lasting importance came from a comment Jesus said: "You are Peter [*Kepha* in Aramaic], and on this rock [*kepha* in Aramaic] I will build my church" (Matthew 16:18). Peter's task of evangelizing Jews kept his focus on works while Paul's task of evangelizing Gentiles kept his focus on faith. The tension between Gentile faith and Jewish works can be seen throughout the entire Christian Sequel as expressions of either Pauline theology or Petrine theology.

For example, the gospel of Matthew shows an obvious Petrine influence: "Everyone then who hears these words of mine and acts on them will be like a wise man who built his house on *rock*" (Matthew 7:24). *See Appendix B for the context of the Christian Sequel authors.* The rock solid foundation of the Jewish scriptures was the heart and soul of messianic Judaism, but obedience to the law took a beating by Jesus who routinely broke the law. The early church would gradually find its way through these troubled waters by recognizing their unique understanding of monotheism in the light of Jesus the Christ who came for all.

A Natural History of Scripture

Paul and His Epistles

Paul was a devout Jew who never met Jesus, but had an experience with the resurrected Jesus (Acts 9:1-19). Paul later wrote that after the resurrection, Jesus "appeared to Cephas [Peter], then to the twelve [disciples]. Then he appeared to more than five hundred brothers and sisters at one time, most of whom are still alive, though some have died. Then he appeared to James, then to all the apostles. Last of all, as to one untimely born, he appeared also to me" (1 Corinthians 15:5-7). Although Paul shared little about himself, his biography was recorded in Acts.[60]

Here are a few more introductory thoughts about Paul:

- Paul (originally known as Saul) offered the first theology for the Church, by way of interpreting the Jesus experience in letters to friends.
- Paul's theology concerned the cross and everything he talked about came from that perspective.
- Paul wrote his letters before the Gospels were written. This simple reality of chronology is rarely thought about, but it gives his letters great importance because they were written down closer to the Christ event than the Gospels themselves.
- Paul, as well as Jesus, worked from an open canon for scripture because the canonization process was not completed until well after their deaths.

Paul's letters reinterpreted the Jewish covenant to include Gentiles, at a time in history when dozens of documents attempted to redefine the covenant, e.g. the Dead

A Natural History of Scripture

Sea Scrolls, the Pseudepigrapha, the Apocrypha, and the yet-to-be canonized Writings section of the Hebrew scriptures. This era was the "most inventive, most imaginative, most ideationally fecund in matters of religion of any time that is adequately recorded in human history."[61]

Paul's ideas were thought to have lasting value and significance for all churches, and his writing served to bridge the growing geographical distance as the gospel spread. Scholars have shown that there are two bodies of work within the Pauline Epistles. The first group is known as the uncontested epistles because their authorship by Paul is undoubted. The second group is known as the deutero-Pauline writings because their authorship by Paul is doubted. This is not to say someone was being fraudulent. A disciple of Paul would certainly want to invoke Pauline authority when responding to a problem after the death of Paul.

1 Thessalonians

This epistle settles in as the earliest preserved Christian writing. Paul was spreading the gospel message to the Gentiles on the Asian continent when he had a vision of a man pleading him to come over to the European continent (Acts 16:9). His first stop was in Philippi where he was shamefully treated (1 Thessalonians 2:2). He then proceeded across the Via Egnatia, the ancient Roman road that connected the two continents, and arrived in Thessalonica.

Having visited many of the cities mentioned in Paul's letters, I found it interesting that most are in ruins today while

A Natural History of Scripture

the modern city of Thessaloniki still thrives. It is not known how long Paul stayed there, but he mentions that he worked night and day to keep from becoming a financial burden while he proclaimed the gospel (1 Thessalonians 2:9). Once a church was established there, he moved on. Hearing of problems and concerns, Paul sent this letter to them through Timothy. Although he was in Athens at the time (1 Thessalonians 3:1), most scholars believe Paul composed this letter from his residence in Corinth.

Galatians

Paul had established churches in Galatia during his first and second missionary journeys. To say the least, this epistle vents anger that he is now considered an enemy (Galatians 4:16). Messianic Jews had come to Galatia and convinced the Gentiles that they needed to become Jews first by obeying the Torah, and then become messianic Jews.

The background story for this epistle is one of defense. Paul is creating a courtroom atmosphere with the Torah-following messianic Jews "as the accusers, Paul as the defendant, and the Galatians as the judge."[62] He offers six arguments to convince the Galatians that salvation comes through faith and that the works of the Torah will not bring them salvation. Most scholars believe Paul was living in Ephesus when he composed this angry letter.

Philemon

This letter is about freedom in Christ, made concrete in

A Natural History of Scripture

the social arena. Onesimus was Philemon's slave who ran away, was evangelized by Paul, and returned to Philemon on equal terms as a free person in Christ (Philemon 17). Paul has already taken the stand that in Christ Jesus "there is neither slave nor free" (Galatians 3:28), because the theology of freedom works itself out in a culture of equality. The letter is all the more powerful because Paul wrote it from prison, probably while he was in Ephesus.

Philippians

Today this city stands in ruins. In Paul's day it was a major Roman city and it was where Paul established his first church on European soil some six years previous. Continuing his themes of freedom, slavery, and equality, Paul then showed Jesus as a slave to be imitated:

> Let the same mind be in you that was in Christ Jesus, who, though he was in the form of God, did not regard equality with God as something to be exploited, but emptied himself, taking the form of a slave, being born in human likeness. And being found in human form, he humbled himself and became obedient to the point of death—even death on a cross (Philippians 2:5-8).

Since this text is one of the most famous passages ever penned by the apostle, let me finish it:

> Therefore God also highly exalted him and gave him the name that is above every name, so

A Natural History of Scripture

that at the name of Jesus every knee should bend, in heaven and on earth and under the earth, and every tongue should confess that Jesus Christ is Lord, to the glory of God the Father (Philippians 2:9-11).

This epistle was also written from prison while Paul was in Ephesus.

1 Corinthians

When the Roman Emperor Claudius ordered the expulsion of the Jews from Rome in AD 49, many settled in Corinth and built a synagogue there. This is where Paul preached that Jesus was the Messiah and eventually started a church of Jewish and Gentile converts (Acts 18:1-4). These people were no doubt an eclectic group of troubled folk, making his Corinthian correspondence especially applicable for us today.

His first letter to the people of Corinth was written while he was still in Ephesus, and much had taken place since his visit to Corinth in AD 50-51. Paul had previously written them (1 Corinthians 5:9, now lost), and his current letter was in response to questions they had (1 Corinthians 7:1). This letter contains the famous love chapter (1 Corinthians 13) and "1 Corinthians 10:14-22 and 11:17-34 are extraordinarily important as the only references to the eucharist in the Pauline letters and also the oldest preserved written eucharistic testimony."[63]

A Natural History of Scripture

2 Corinthians

Paul must have gotten word that things were not going well in Corinth, so he made a second visit to the city (2 Corinthians 13:2), which turned out to be a failure. He left Corinth with the intention of returning, but changed his mind and wrote another letter from Ephesus (2 Corinthians 2:4, also lost) instead of making "another painful visit" (2 Corinthians 2:1). He then left Ephesus and traveled to Macedonia (Acts 20:1), where he got word from Titus that attitudes among the Corinthians had greatly improved toward Paul (2 Corinthians 7:5-7).

Paul then composed 2 Corinthians, while in Macedonia, asking the people of Corinth to take a collection for the poor in Jerusalem. Paul himself finally returned to Corinth for a third time (2 Corinthians 13:1) where he spent the winter of AD 57-58. He then took the collection to Jerusalem by way of Macedonia and Troas (Acts 20:2-5).

Romans

Before leaving Corinth, Paul wrote a letter to the Romans, which not only provided his final work but also conveyed the full maturity of his thought. Others established the Roman churches, so Paul wanted to encourage them himself, with a summary of his theology. In Romans 1:17 Paul quoted Habakkuk 2:4, but a quick check in your New Revised Standard Version of the Bible shows that it isn't an exact quote. This mystery is resolved if you check the Septuagint, which provides a match.

A Natural History of Scripture

This gives an important point: Christianity did not rise from the Hebrew Scriptures, it rose from the Septuagint.

The Q Gospel

In the nineteenth century, scholars found that Matthew and Luke independently followed Mark's outline of the gospel and supplemented it with teachings from a supposed "Q" source. The discovery of Q did not come from an archaeological dig; it was found buried within the lines of the Gospels.

The solution to the mystery of Q began in Germany during the 1830s. Contrary to centuries of church tradition, which ranked Matthew as the oldest gospel, some historians proposed that Matthew and Luke had copied from the gospel of Mark. In 1838, Christian Weisse, a lecturer at the University of Leipzig, suggested that Matthew and Luke had drawn not only from Mark, but also from an unknown source. Laying Matthew and Luke side by side, Weisse realized that this other source was filled with sayings of Jesus that did not appear in Mark. It soon became known as 'Q', drawing its name from the German word *Quelle*, which means source. A classic example is Matthew 3:7-10 and Luke 3:7-9. Those passages have over sixty words in Greek that are almost verbatim the same in Matthew and Luke and they do not appear in Mark.

Most scholars believe that Matthew and Luke were unaware of each other's gospel, so their common material had to come from an earlier written source to which they both had access. The Q Gospel has since proven to be the original source for over 225 verses in Matthew and Luke.

A Natural History of Scripture

See the next several pages for the parallel Matthew and Luke verses that came from Q.[64]

The Q Gospel

Q Saying	Matthew Parallel	Luke Parallel
1	3:1-3	3:2b-4
2	3:5-10	3:7-11
3		3:12-14
4	3:11-12	3:16-17
5	3:13,16-17	3:21b-22
6	4:1-4	4:1-4
7	4:5-7	4:9-12
8	4:8-11	4:5-8,13
9	5:1-2,3,6	6:12,17,20-21
10	5:6;5:4	6:21
11	5:5	
12	5:7-9	
13	5:11-12	6:22-23
14	5:44,46	6:27-28
15	5:39b-42	6:29-30
16	7:12;5:46-47	6:31-33,35b
17	5:48	6:36
18	7:1-2	6:38
19	15:14;10:24-25	6:39-40
20	7:3-5	6:41-42
21	7:16-20;12:35	6:43-45
22	7:21-27	6:46-49
23	8:5-13	7:1b-10

A Natural History of Scripture

24	11:2-11	7:18-20,22-28
25	11:12-13	16:16
26	11:16-19	7:31-35
27	8:19-22	9:57-60
28	10:16;9:37	10:2-3
29	10:9-10	9:3;10:4
30	10:11-12	10:5-9
31	10:40;11:21-23	10:10-12,13-16
32	11:25-27	10:21-22
33	13:16-17	10:23-24
34	6:9-13	11:1-4
35	7:7-8	11:9-11
36	7:9-11	11:11-13
37	12:22-28	11:14-20
38	12:30	11:23
39	12:43-45	11:24-26
40		11:27-28
41	12:38-42	11:16,29-32
42	5:15;16:22-23	11:33-36
43	23:23,26	11:39-42
44	23:6-7,29-35	11:43-51
45	10:26-27	12:2-3
46	10:28-31	12:4-7
47	10:32	12:8
48	10:19-20;12:32	12:9-12
49		12:13-14
50		12:16-21
51	6:25-27	12:22-26
52	6:28-30	12:27-28
53	6:21-33	12:29-31
54	6:19-21	12:33-34

A Natural History of Scripture

55	24:42-44	12:39-40
56	24:45-51	12:42-46
57	10:34-36	12:51-53
58	10:39	17:33
59	16:2-3	12:54-56
60	5:25-26	12:57-59
61	3:31-32	13:18-19
62	13:33	13:20-21
63	7:13-14	13:24
64	8:11-12	13:28-29
65	20:16	13:30
66	23:37-39	13:34-35
67	23:12	14:11
68	22:1-10	14:16-24
69	10:37-38	14:26-27
70	5:13	14:34-35
71	18:12-13	15:4-7
72		15:8-10
73	6:24	16:13
74	5:18	16:17
75	5:32	16:18
76	18:6-7	17:1-2
77	18:15,21-22	17:3-4
78	17:20	17:6
79		17:20-21
80	24:26,37-41	17:22-26,34
81	25:14-30	19:12-23
82	19:28	22:28-30

Figure 7

A Natural History of Scripture

The First Jewish Revolt and the Destruction of the Second Temple

Tensions had run high between the Romans and the Jews throughout the past century. Things began coming to a head in AD 66 when the Romans stole large amounts of silver from the temple. The outraged Jews responded with a great revolt. Having some minor successes, the Jews believed they could ultimately defeat the Romans and finally win back control of their promised land. To that end they began killing fellow Jews who were not sympathetic to the cause. Rabbi Yohanan ben Zakkai arranged to have himself removed from Jerusalem inside a coffin. Safely outside he surrendered to the Romans who allowed him to reestablish Jewish communal life in the town of Jamnia.

On the ninth day of the Hebrew month of Av, AD 70, the Romans torched the temple and nearly burned it to the ground. The only thing that remained was the Western Wall of the temple, which remains today. Having visited the Western Wall twice, I can testify that it is a profound religious experience to pray at that holy site. After the destruction of the second temple, nearly a thousand surviving Jewish rebels fled to the natural fortress of Masada. The Romans set up a siege because they knew this group of rebels was responsible for starting the revolt in the first place.

As it became apparent that the Romans would not lose this battle, the Jews made a pact to commit suicide rather than become enslaved to the Romans. The historian Josephus wrote that in AD 73 the Romans advanced to the wall over gangways, expecting fierce resistance. But no enemy appeared, and an awful silence hung over the place. They

A Natural History of Scripture

finally shouted in their perplexity, to arouse anyone. Hearing the noise, the two women who had saved themselves came out of hiding and informed the Romans of what had happened.[65]

Mark

Paul knew that the geographical distance needed bridged, from the beginnings of the gospel in Israel to its spread in Europe. The problem now was the chronological distance, so the evangelists wrote to keep the stories alive. Mark was the first evangelist to write, and his account of the gospel was deeply colored by the Roman persecution of messianic Jews. Mark may have been the John Mark mentioned in Acts 12:12, and the gospel was probably written in Rome.

Rome was going through its own turmoil at this time in history. After Nero died in AD 68, four emperors replaced him over the course of the next year, settling with Vespasian in AD 69. The infamous persecution of the so-called 'Christians' in Rome, where legend says both Peter and Paul perished, set the scene for the writing of the gospel of Mark. Mark was a Greek-speaking Jew who spent time with Peter and Paul and now his task was to share the stories passed down through the apostolic tradition. Tradition says it was a summary of Peter's preaching.

Mark was not an eyewitness of the life of Jesus, but his direct experience with Peter and Paul gave him credibility as an author. The title of "The Gospel According to Mark" was not original and was probably added by the end of the second

A Natural History of Scripture

century. Mark's account also has later additions at the end his gospel. Mark originally ended with "So they went out and fled from the tomb, for terror and amazement had seized them; and they said nothing to anyone, for they were afraid" (Mark 16:8). This ending expressed the feelings that overwhelmed the Roman messianic Jews who were in the midst of their own local fears and horrors. Later editors added new endings to balance the majesty and mystery of the full Jesus story.

*This would be a good time
to stop and explore
Guided Exercise #6
on the next page.*

A Natural History of Scripture

Guided Exercise #6

As scholars first began to solve the mystery of who Mark was, they began to notice that the author of the gospel of Mark seemed to have confusion about Palestinian geography. This is part of the reason that scholars today believe Mark was not an eyewitness of the Jesus event. Bearing in mind that my own mother can get lost in her hometown, look at the following geographical problems in Mark:

1. <u>Mark 5:1, 13</u>. I have been to the site where the pigs ran down the steep embankment and drowned in the Sea of Galilee (vs. 13). The problem is that Mark locates the scene in Gerasa (vs. 1), which is over thirty miles away from the sea.

2. <u>Mark 6:45, 53</u>. In verse 45, Jesus tells his disciples to go to Bethsaida, on the northeast side of the Sea of Galilee. When they arrive (vs. 53), they are at Gennesaret, which is on the northwest side of the sea.

3. <u>Mark 7:31</u>. This verse reports Jesus' return from Tyre to the Sea of Galilee by way of Sidon. This could happen, but it is extremely unnatural because Sidon is north of Tyre and Galilee is southeast.

4. <u>Mark 8:10</u>. No one has been able to locate the district of Dalmanutha. Mark may have been referring to Magdala, but not knowing the region he offered a misspelling of the name.

A Natural History of Scripture

Christianity

The Romans were the first to give the messianic Jews the distinctive name of Christians. A Christian was simply a Christ follower, and Christ was the Greek way to say the Hebrew word *messiah*. This is where Christianity started breaking from Judaism. The Jews had never really developed much of an interest in messianism, and now the Jews and Gentiles who believed Jesus was the messiah were going in a very different direction. Messiah simply meant 'anointed' and the prophetic part of the Hebrew Scriptures used the term to describe the ceremony for anointing kings.

Since the Jews believed the ideal messiah would be a human, as all other Hebrew kings had been, the Christian claim of Jesus' divinity became an early wedge that drove the two religions apart. The inclusion of Gentiles was the next big difference that kept the two groups growing in separate directions. How could a proper Jew attend synagogue with an unclean person? Gentiles were uncircumcised people who ate pork and did not need to follow Torah.

A change was needed because some "Jews had already agreed that anyone who confessed Jesus to be the Messiah would be put out of the synagogue" (John 9:22). Christians followed the example from their Jewish heritage of meeting in homes when the temple was destroyed. The early church grew in spite of persecution from Jews and Romans alike, and rumors flourished that Christians were cannibals and caused natural disasters due to angering the Roman gods.

A Natural History of Scripture

Various Letters

1 Peter

If this letter were written by Simon Peter, we would have a book authored by an eyewitness of Jesus. However, most scholars believe this letter was written in Rome by a disciple of Peter, sometime soon after the destruction of the temple, for some of the following reasons:

1) "Babylon" (1 Peter 5:13) was a popular name for Rome after the destruction of the temple.

2) "elder" (1 Peter 5:1) was a term from church organization that had not developed until after Peter's lifetime.

3) "Honor the emperor" (1 Peter 2:17) would make sense during the reign of Vespasian (AD 68-78), but not during Nero's persecution (AD 64-68), nor the final year's of Domitian's Reign (AD 81-96).

James

This letter was written to messianic Jews living outside the Holy Land, or as the writer put it, "To the twelve tribes in the Dispersion" (James 1:1). The author wrote sometime in the

A Natural History of Scripture

80s or 90s and invoked the name of James, the leader of the early church, to lend authority to the hearing of his letter. Paul's letters had been circulating for twenty to thirty years by this time, and his glowing defense of the sufficiency of faith was creating misunderstandings. The author of James offered a corrective by writing that "a person is justified by works and not by faith alone" (James 2:24). This letter is remarkably similar to Matthew's Sermon on the Mount, meaning the teachings probably came from a document similar to the Q gospel.

Colossians

Scholars are divided on the authorship of this book. Significant differences between this letter and unquestionably authentic Pauline letters, has caused a small majority of scholars to take the stance that Colossians was written by one of Paul's students. If this theory is right, the letter was written in Paul's name in the eighties from Ephesus. The purpose of the letter was to attack false teachings that had developed in the natural course of this Greek-influenced, Gentile community.

Hebrews

The author of this magnificent treatise is unknown, but it was probably written in the eighties from Rome. The heart of this letter concerned the sacrifice of Jesus, which the author said, "is hard to explain" (Hebrews 5:11). Paul had written to the Romans a generation earlier about freedom from the Law, and this book appears to be building on that foundation. This author said, "if that first covenant had been faultless, there would have been no need to look for a second one" (Hebrews 8:7). While the title of Hebrews can be misleading, it is worthwhile to mention that the title is not original.

Jude

The author of this letter actually called himself Judas, but translators traditionally shorten the name to Jude so readers won't confuse the writer with Judas the betrayer. The name Judas was probably used to identify the writer as one of the four brothers of Jesus (Mark 6:3), which would also make him the "brother of James" (Jude 1). The letter was probably sent from Palestine in the 90s to churches influenced by the Palestinian churches. Intriguingly, Jude quotes from Enoch (Jude 14-15), which was not then and never has been, considered a canonical work.

Ephesians

An Ephesian disciple of Paul probably wrote this letter sometime in the nineties. It is remarkably similar to the thematic progression of Colossians, which was written some

A Natural History of Scripture

ten years earlier in Ephesus. This means that the unknown author of Ephesians probably used the Pauline thought in Colossians as a model for his letter. While the previous letter had the purpose of attacking false teachings, Ephesians was written to redevelop Pauline theology for a new place and time. Newness between Jews and Gentiles was evidenced in the author's discussion of Christ: "For he is our peace; in his flesh he has made both groups into one and has broken down the dividing wall, that is, the hostility between us" (Ephesians 2:14).

2 Thessalonians

This letter was written by an unknown author who modeled his thought after Paul's letter to the Thessalonians. This new letter was needed to address a dispute toward the end of the century, about the second coming of Christ: "As to the coming of our Lord Jesus Christ and our being gathered together to him, we beg you, brothers and sisters, not to be quickly shaken in mind or alarmed, either by spirit or by word or by letter, as though from us, to the effect that the day of the Lord is already here" (2 Thessalonians 2:1-2).

Closing of the Hebrew Bible

Judaism was certainly no longer the same. The temple was destroyed, the land was not theirs, and Gentiles were allowed into the Jewish movement that had finally developed

A Natural History of Scripture

into Christianity. The Jews that didn't believe Jesus was the Messiah had to entrench. They chose to study their scriptures, become people of the book, and teach. This gave birth to rabbinic Judaism. One of their first tasks was to choose which books among the hundreds of writings would join the Law and the Prophets as canonized.

The fact is we do not know for sure how the final selection process took place. Two theories have lingered the longest, but they take canonization as an event rather than a process. The first theory focuses on a restoration movement in Jamnia, led by Rabban Yohanan ben Zakkai. What took place at Jamnia were debates. One of the debates concerned the status of five biblical books: Ecclesiastes, Song of Songs, Ezekiel, Proverbs, and Esther. There is no indication that these five books faced widespread objections and there is little evidence that the so-called Council of Jamnia made a declaration about which books were canonical and which were not.

The second theory assumes the Jews who had settled in Alexandria after the exile had a wider canon, and that early Christians simply accepted this list. The Greek Bible, or Septuagint, was the Bible of the early Christians, but the earliest full manuscripts of the Septuagint are varied in their contents. This makes it impossible to determine canonical status. The sensational discovery of the Dead Sea Scrolls in the caves of Qumran gave scholars hope for new understanding. Manuscripts of all the Hebrew Scriptures (except Esther) have been found there, but so have many other documents. It is not at all clear if the Qumran Essenes distinguished between canonical and noncanonical books.

A Natural History of Scripture

The Dead Sea discoveries prove only that the canonical books were very important to the Essenes. From other Jewish sources we know that by the late first century AD there was a distinction between canonical and noncanonical books. What probably happened at Jamnia was the informal adoption of a canon that the community had already accepted. This effectively censored all other writings, including the letters of Paul and the gospel stories about Jesus. This new Writings section of the Hebrew Scriptures had various books that were still being debated by rabbis in the third and fourth centuries AD, but "no additions to the biblical canon were made after the first century."[66]

Many scholars today are accepting the process notion of canonization. The Law must have gained canonical status by the sixth century BC when Ezra the scribe was told to "bring the book of the law of Moses, which the LORD had given to Israel" (Nehemiah 8:1). The Prophets achieved canonical status over the next four centuries, and the Writings were canonized by AD 100. As the Hebrew Bible closed, it became known as a tripartite canon, recognizing the differences between the Law, the Prophets, and the Writings sections. The foundations for this had been laid long ago: "For instruction [the Law] shall not perish from the priest, nor counsel [the Writings] from the wise, nor the word from the prophet [the Prophets]" (Jeremiah 18:18).

*See Appendix A for the context of
the Hebrew Scriptures.*

Matthew

A Natural History of Scripture

The unknown author who wrote Matthew, probably composed it around AD 90 from Antioch. While Mark wrote from an environment of fear, Matthew wrote from an environment of division. The division was over the deepening rift that had produced church as separate from synagogue, and Matthew was telling his readers that it was time to complete the break. His gospel presented both the legal and prophetic writings of the Hebrew scriptures as being fulfilled in Christ.

Matthew's gospel blossomed first as the fulfillment of the Law. This idea was implicit in the presentation of five teachings,[67] designed to imitate the five books of the Law, and Jesus was presented as the new lawgiver. Just as Moses went up Mount Sinai to receive the Law (Exodus 19:20), Jesus went up a mountain to deliver a new Law (Matthew 5:1), which has come to be known as the Sermon on the Mount. In that teaching, Jesus said "Do not think that I have come to abolish the law or the prophets; I have come not to abolish but to fulfill" (Matthew 5:17).

Matthew's gospel blossomed next as the fulfillment of prophecy. He seemed to go out of his way to make connections between Jesus and the prophets of old, as can be seen in the following stories: Matthew 4:12-16; 8:14-17; 12:15-21; 13:34-35; 21:1-5; 27:3-10. Matthew's Jewishness is especially noticed in his preference for the term 'Kingdom of Heaven.' The other gospels used the term 'Kingdom of God,' but Matthew was "more alert to Jewish sensitivities about 'the Name' and therefore less willing to seem to speak casually of 'God'."[68]

This would be a good time to pursue Guided Exercise #7 on the next page.

A Natural History of Scripture

Guided Exercise #7

Matthew's gospel originally started with Chapter 3, but the popularity of Jesus probably caused people to want to know about his birth. The first two chapters were later appended to the beginning of the story to share this information. Matthew continued his style of searching scripture to let the prophecies of old become fulfilled in the birth of Jesus.

1. Matthew 1:18-23. The prophecy in verse 23 is from Isaiah 7:14. The word 'virgin' does not show up in the Hebrew text of Isaiah 7:14—it reads 'young woman.' Matthew was quoting from the Greek translation of the Hebrew, known as the Septuagint, which chose the Greek word for virgin rather than the Greek word for young woman.
2. Matthew 2:13-15. The prophecy in verse 15 is from Hosea 11:1. The Hosea text actually mentions that the 'son' God called out of Egypt was Israel. How successful do you think this proof text was for the people of Antioch to believe it was about Jesus?
3. Matthew 2:16-18. The prophecy in verse 18 is from Jeremiah 31:15. The grief expressed in the Jeremiah passage concerns the exile of the northern tribes. How does this proof text work for you?
4. Matthew 2:19-23. The prophecy in verse 23 simply does not exist in the Hebrew Scriptures. There is a vague connection between Nazorean, Nazereth, and the Hebrew word for shoot in Isaiah 11:1, but Matthew seems to be pushing the envelope here for connections.

A Natural History of Scripture

Luke/Acts

Luke was probably a Gentile who converted to Christianity. His strong command of Greek makes it possible that he wrote from Greece around AD 90 to the churches Paul founded there. He was not an eyewitness of Jesus, so his gospel was written to "set down an orderly account of the events that have been fulfilled among us, just as they were handed on to us by those who from the beginning were eyewitnesses and servants of the word" (Luke 1:1-2).

Luke's Gentile status shows up in many ways. He is the only Christian Sequel author to reject the Jewish word 'rabbi' and instead use the Greek equivalent word 'master' (Luke 5:5) when referring to Jesus. His desire not to offend Gentile sensibilities showed up when Jesus said from the cross "Father, forgive them; for they do not know what they are doing" (Luke 23:34), Luke was also the only one to report Jesus' response to one of the Gentile criminals hanging with him: "Truly I tell you, today you will be with me in Paradise" (Luke 23:43).

Acts is volume 2 of Luke's magisterial work (Acts 1:1). It picks up after the resurrection of Jesus and concludes with Paul in Rome "proclaiming the kingdom of God and teaching about the Lord Jesus Christ with all boldness and without hindrance" (Acts 28:31). Nearly thirty years of history are recorded in this book, which testifies to an incredibly small window of understanding shed on the development of the early Church.

A Natural History of Scripture

Revelation

The author of this book was probably a Jewish Christian prophet named John, who left Palestine during the First Jewish War and was ultimately exiled to Patmos (Revelation 1:9). Sometime in the mid 90s, the author was having a prophetic vision when he heard a loud voice say "Write in a book what you see and send it to the seven churches, to Ephesus, to Smyrna, to Pergamum, to Thyatira, to Sardis, to Philadelphia, and to Laodicea" (Revelation 1:11).

What John saw was indescribable, so he called upon familiar images from the Hebrew Scriptures to put the vision into words. Of the book's 404 verses, there were 518 allusions to the Hebrew prophets. The images were symbolic so that the letters might not get intercepted by the Romans and destroyed. Roman persecution of Christians was localized in Rome during Nero's reign, but it was spreading throughout the Roman Empire toward the end of Domitian's reign (AD 81—AD 96).

The number of the beast (Revelation 13:8) referred to Nero, but he was long dead by this time. The Christians of the seven churches had hoped the evil reign of Nero was over, but it was resurrected in the evil reign of Domitian. John symbolically explained this with the imagery of a seven-headed dragon: "One of its heads seemed to have received a death-blow, but its mortal wound had been healed" (Revelation 13:3).

The book was offered to suffering Christians as a vision of hope and final victory. Encouragement was shared with believers by revealing what awaited them in heaven (Revelation 7:9-17). The symbolism of this book has led to even more imaginative interpretations. With the recent destruction of the World Trade Center, it might be good to note that "God has not revealed to human beings details about how the world began or how the world will end, and failing to recognize that, one is likely to misread both the first book and the last book in the Bible."[69]

John

The unknown author of John probably wrote this gospel from Ephesus. He was probably a disciple of John who recorded the preaching of John in the same manner that Mark recorded the preaching of Peter. While tradition has labeled the other three gospels 'synoptic,' meaning one eye or similar, this gospel simply adds more theological insights into the oral stories of Jesus than do the others. For instance, there are many 'I Am' statements which serve the purpose of making Jesus divine, because 'I Am' is the Greek translation of God's Hebrew name from Exodus 3:14.

A particularly telling example of this formula comes in the reaction by Jesus' arrest party:

> Then Jesus, knowing all that was to happen to him, came forward and asked them, 'Whom are you looking for?' They answered, 'Jesus of Nazareth.' Jesus replied, 'I am he.' Judas, who betrayed him, was standing with them. When Jesus said to them, 'I am he,' *they stepped back and fell to the ground* [author's italics]. Again he asked them,

A Natural History of Scripture

'Whom are you looking for?' And they said, 'Jesus of Nazareth.' Jesus answered, 'I told you that I am he. So if you are looking for me, let these men go' (John 18:4-8).

The theological nature of this gospel can also be seen in its thematic construction. As synagogue and church continued to find separate identities (synagogue rallied around the Law and church rallied around the Gospel), John showed Jesus as the fulfillment and transformation of the Jewish Festivals. The Feast of Tabernacles (John 7:2) began with the lighting of golden lamps in the temple, and during this event John's Jesus announced "I am the light of the world" (John 8:12).

The Feast of Dedication (John 10:22) remembered the sanctification of the temple desecrated during the Macabbean revolt, and during this event John's Jesus announced he was "the one sanctified and sent into the world" (John 10:36). The Feast of Passover[70] celebrated, among other things, the manna from heaven during the exodus, and during this event John's Jesus announced "I am the bread of life" (John 6:35).

Editing is also noticeable in this gospel. The earliest manuscripts we have of John do not have the passage about the woman caught in adultery (John 7:53-8:11). Not only did a later editor add in this story, but it also interrupted a seven scene poetic construction around Jesus as the water and light of life. The original ending shows the author's purpose: "But these are written so that you may come to believe that Jesus is the Messiah, the Son of God, and that through believing you may have life in his name" (John 20:31). A later editor then appended an epilogue (John 21:1-25).

A Natural History of Scripture

Different Perspectives

It has long been noticed that the Synoptic Gospels (Matthew, Mark, and Luke) are significantly different from the gospel of John. This is due in part to the fact that the Synoptics chose to focus on the historical Jesus, while John dealt more with the theological Jesus. Prior to the Gospels, Paul showed virtually no interest in the Jesus of history, because his concern was with the Christ of faith. He even went so far as to say that Easter was what made Jesus divine, not the cross, his baptism, or his birth. Paul explained that Jesus was declared "to be Son of God with power according to the spirit of holiness by resurrection from the dead" (Romans 1:4).

This same elevation of Jesus as the Christ occurs in Acts, but he is portrayed historically rather than theologically:

> Jesus of Nazareth, a man attested to you by God with deeds of power, wonders, and signs that God did through him among you, as you yourselves know—this man, handed over to you according to the definite plan and foreknowledge of God, you crucified and killed by the hands of those outside the law. But God raised him up, having freed him from death, because it was impossible for him to be held in its power (Acts 2:22-24).

This gives us four different perspectives of Jesus. Easter is not so much the dividing line between the Jesus of history and the Christ of faith, as it is the center point from which radiates four perspectives.

A Natural History of Scripture

*Inspired by thoughts
from Geza Vermes'
The Changing Faces of Jesus,*[71]
*I created a chart on
the Jesus of history
and the Christ of faith
which can be found
on the next page.
It shows four quadrants
with their associated author(s).*

A Natural History of Scripture

Jesus of History/Christ of Faith

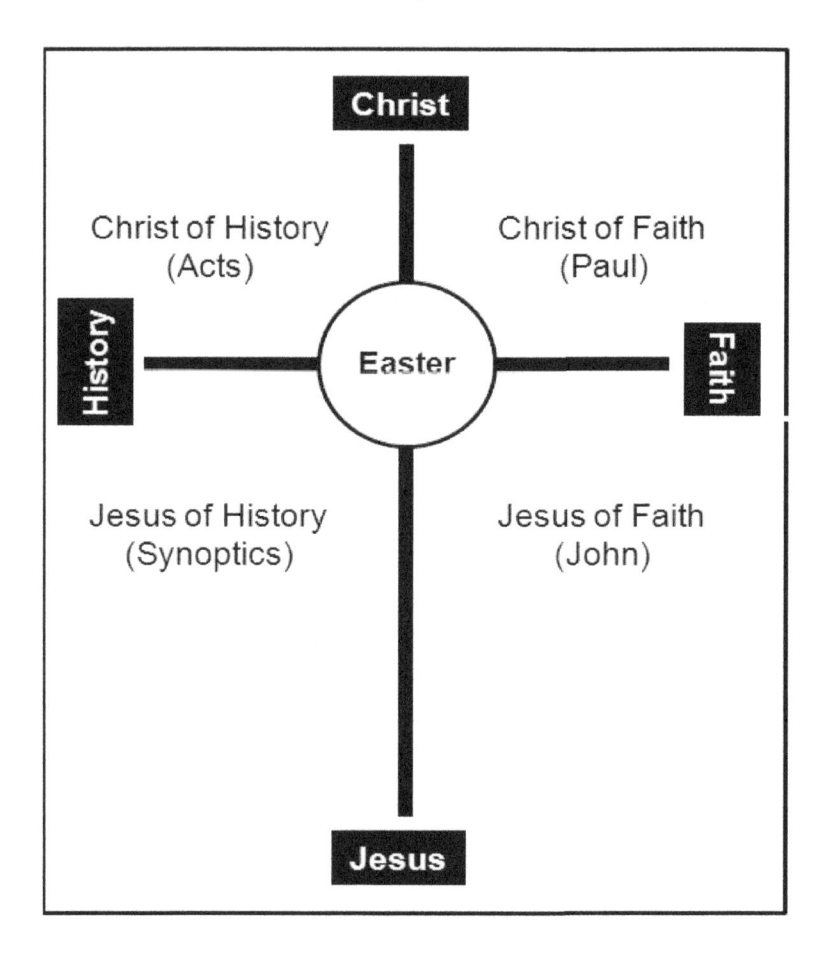

Christ

Christ of History (Acts) — Christ of Faith (Paul)

History — Easter — **Faith**

Jesus of History (Synoptics) — Jesus of Faith (John)

Jesus

Figure 8

A Natural History of Scripture

Part Four
Adult Stage: Standardizers

Prenatal Stage: Storytellers	Infant Stage: Writers		Adolescent Stage: Editors			Adult Stage: Standardizers	
Oral History	Written History	Pro-phets	Priests	Trans-lators	Evan-gelists	Politi-cians	Pub-lishers

2000 BC   950 BC   750 BC 586 BC   332 BC   63 BC   AD 144   AD 1454   NOW

Monsters are almost certainly misfits that will be swept away by the power of natural selection.[72]

The first three parts of this book show the evolution of the canon of the Bible through developmental changes in its words. Part Four, The Adult Stage, considers the evolutionary processes occurring above (macroevolution) and below (microevolution) the story level. While Politicians worked to standardize the big picture of the biblical canon, publishers attempted to standardize the variations within the text.

A Natural History of Scripture

Chapter 7 shows how politicians became the agents of selection that led to the canonization of the Christian sequel. This process continues today as exemplified in the rediscovery of the gnostic texts. Although much acclaim has gone to this find, we would do well to listen to the field of evolutionary development and its understanding that misfits do not give rise to a new species. Chapter 8 explains how publishers continue to pursue a standardization of the text.

A Natural History of Scripture

Chapter 7
Politicians: Natural Selection in Process

Prenatal Stage: Storytellers	Infant Stage: Writers		Adolescent Stage: Editors			Adult Stage: Standardizers	
Oral History	Written History	Prophets	Priests	Translators	Evangelists	**Politicians**	Publishers
2000 BC	950 BC	750 BC	586 BC	332 BC	63 BC	AD 144	AD 1454 NOW

Canonization is a process, not an event.[73]

Natural selection operates as a principle of success. Politicians became the agents of selection that led to the canonization of the successful stories of the Christian sequel. This took place through a series of events: the natural rejection and death of the weaker stories of Marcionism and Gnosticism; the adaptive stories of the Jewish Mishna, the Muslim sequel, and the Jewish Talmuddim; the

A Natural History of Scripture

varietal stories of the Apocrypha; and the gradualism of the Council of Nicaea.

The Second Century

1, 2, 3 John

A disciple of John around AD 100 probably composed these three letters: First John was written to a group of churches; Second John was written to an individual church; Third John was written to an individual. Although the author of 1 John took a hard core stance for love (1 John 4:8), he also refused to pray for people who commit a mortal sin (1 John 5:16). A passage in 2 John cautioned a church to be wary of false teachers (2 John 7) and not even show them hospitality (2 John 10). Third John cautioned a friend (3 John 1) to be wary of an over-zealous control freak (3 John 9-10).

Titus

A disciple of Paul around AD 100 probably wrote this letter from Rome, to a disciple of Paul in Crete. The letter helped organize and define early church governance by explaining the qualifications of "elder," meaning mature, and "bishop," meaning overseer (Titus 1:5-9). This represented a major shift from apostolic leadership, because the apostles of the early church were dying off. Once again the church turned

A Natural History of Scripture

to its Jewish heritage for guidance, and found the synagogue model of leadership by the wise among them, which the church called presbyters.

1 Timothy

A disciple of Paul around AD 100 probably wrote this letter from Rome, to a disciple of Paul in Ephesus. The concern was over church problems, which needed resolved many decades after the death of Paul. Such answers as "I permit no woman to teach or to have authority over a man; she is to keep silent" (1 Timothy 2:12) are not the thoughts of Paul, but a much later follower who tried to update Pauline theology for the current church.

2 Timothy

A disciple of Paul around AD 100 probably wrote this letter from Rome, also to a disciple of Paul in Ephesus. It is much more personal in nature than 1 Timothy and contains the famous words "All scripture is inspired by God" (2 Timothy 3:16). A more literal translation of the original Greek would read "Every God-breathed writing," which may reflect an anti-Jewish sentiment. While the verse obviously refers to the Hebrew Scriptures, because the Christian Sequel was still hundreds of years away from being canonized, it may also be complaining about the Jewish attitude against the developing Christian Sequel.

A Natural History of Scripture

The canonization of the Writings section of the Hebrew Bible and the consequential closing of the Hebrew Bible took place in the midst of Paul's circulating letters and the writing down of the gospel stories. The Jewish effort may well have been a response designed to exclude Christian material. If this is so, then the author of 2 Timothy could well have been claiming a God-breathed status for the Christian Sequel as well as the Hebrew Scriptures.

2 Peter

The author of this letter claimed to be the Peter who was on the Mount of Transfiguration with Jesus (2 Peter 1:18), but his claim that Paul's letter's were considered scripture (2 Peter 3:16) testifies to a much later time. Most scholars today believe an unknown author around AD 130 wrote this letter in Rome. It was written to attack false teachers and defend the fading hope of the second coming of Christ. Apocalyptic expectations peaked about AD 100, so the author loosely called upon Psalm 90:4 to explain the lengthy wait for the day of the Lord: "Do not ignore this one fact, beloved, that with the Lord one day is like a thousand years, and a thousand years are like one day" (2 Peter 3:8).

The Second Jewish Revolt

In about AD 130, the Roman emporer Hadrian visited Palestine. To the great dismay of the Jewish inhabitants of Sepphoris, he changed the name of their city to Diocaesarea.

A Natural History of Scripture

To the downright fury of the people of Jerusalem, they heard of Hadrian's plan to rename their city Aelia Capitolina. In AD 132 the Second Jewish War was officially launched. The revolt lasted three years under the leadership of Simon Bar Kosiba.

Reviving messianic expectations, Rabbi Akiba regarded Simon as the "star of David," in fulfillment of Numbers 24:17. Akiba began calling Simon "bar Kochba," meaning "son of a star," but the rebellion met a crushing blow by the Romans in AD 135. Jerusalem was renamed Aelia Capitolina and Judaism was officially outlawed, but three years later it was legalized by the new emperor Antoninus Pius. The academy of rabbis who founded rabbinic Judaism in Jamnia after the first Jewish revolt, now relocated to Galilee.

Important People and Movements

Tatian

Into this swirl of uncanonized letters ultimately headed for the developing Christian Sequel, came an author who started toying with the gospels. Tatian of Mesopotamia wrote a harmony of the four gospels, which had a long-lasting influence. He also began questioning some of the theology of Paul, and wrote books that shared a differing theology from that of the early church. Clearly there were problems that needed addressed, concerning what was scripture and what was not, but the early church had too many problems with organization and administration to settle them.

A Natural History of Scripture

Marcionism

On the Christian front, a wealthy ship owner named Marcion founded Marcionism. He was a member of the Christian community at Rome in the mid-second century who didn't like the Gospels because they incorporated too much of the Hebrew Scriptures. His canon contained only ten letters attributable to Paul and the gospel of Luke, and he rewrote "the story of Jesus and the early church so as to get rid of any Judahist overtones. Thus, he produced the Gospel of Marcion. The actual text has not survived, but it is referred to in other writings of the period."[74] He was probably the first canonical thinker in the Christian faith and he was eventually labeled a heretic for his total rejection of the Hebrew Scriptures.

Gnosticism

Another group that challenged the early development of an orthodox Christian faith was the Gnostics. Gnosticism was a movement in the 2nd and 3rd centuries, which held a deeply dualistic theology between physical and spiritual. Their theology veered from Judaism and their books were ultimately censored from the Christian canon. Their writings were discovered in 1945 in Egypt and are known as the Nag Hammadi Library. This library is "a collection of religious texts that vary widely from each other as to when, where, and by whom they were written."[75] In all, there were thirteen codices consisting of forty-five separate titles. *See the next two pages for a list of the titles.*[76]

A Natural History of Scripture

The Nag Hammadi Library

The Prayer of the Apostle Paul
The Apocryphon of James
The Gospel of Truth
The Treatise on the Resurrection
The Tripartite Tractate
The Apocryphon of John
The Gospel of Thomas
The Gospel of Philip
The Hypostasis of the Archons
On the Origin of the World
The Exegesis on the Soul
The Book of Thomas the Contender
The Gospel of the Egyptians
Eugnostos the Blessed
The Dialogue of the Savior
The Apocalypse of Paul
The First Apocalypse of James
The Second Apocalypse of James
The Apocalypse of Adam
The Acts of Peter and the Twelve Apostles
The Thunder, Perfect Mind
Authoritative Teaching
The Concept of Our Great Power
Plato, Republic
The Discourse on the Eighth and Ninth
The Prayer of Thanksgiving and Scribal Note
Asclepius
The Paraphrase of Shem
The Second Treatise of the Great Seth

A Natural History of Scripture

Apocalypse of Peter
The Teachings of Sylvanus
The Three Steles of Seth
Zostrianos
The Letter of Peter to Phillip
Melchizedek
The Thought of Norea
The Testimony of Truth
Marsanes
The Interpretation of Knowledge
A Valentinian Exposition
Allogenes
Hypsiphrone
The Sentences of Sextus
Fragments
Trimorphic Protennoia
The Gospel of Mary
The Act of Peter

Figure 9

Editing of the Christian Sequel

Although the canonization of the Christian Sequel was still in its early stages, the hand of an editor can already be noticed in the process. Every extant manuscript contains the so-called *nomina sacra*, or sacred names. No matter where the manuscript was found, how old it was, nor the material it was written on, the *nomina sacra* appear in the same abbreviated way. The most common sacred names to get this special

A Natural History of Scripture

treatment were: God, Lord, Jesus, Christ, spirit, man, cross, father, son, redeemer, mother, heaven, Israel, David, and Jerusalem.[77]

Another clue that an editor was working with the Christian Sequel well before its canonization can be found in the titles of the Gospels. The Gospels have the same three-word pattern, each of which is unusual: 1) they start with the word for "Gospel," which is never used within the writings themselves to refer to a literary genre; 2) they continue with the word for "according to," which is extremely rare for book titles; 3) they end with the name of the author, which cannot be derived with certainty from the text.[78]

The Mishnah

As Christians were slowly settling on a new collection of sacred texts, as a sequel to the Hebrew Scriptures, rabbinic Judaism was compiling an oral tradition as an update to Mosaic Law. This was done by a group of scholars known as *tannaim*, and the result of their effort became known as the Mishnah, which means repeat. As these people repeated the old laws and argued over how to update them, they likewise abandoned scriptural references. The decision to focus on right behavior rather than to continue God's story, as the Christians did, probably reflected disappointment about the narratives of exile and temple destruction.

The oral tradition compiled by the *tannaitic* scholars was codified by subject matter in AD 200 by Rabbi Judah. This signified the birth of the Mishnah, which represented nearly 150 sages debating over the course of 523 chapters. The true

A Natural History of Scripture

genius of the Mishna was the updating of laws that concerned the temple. The Rabbis turned each home into a tiny temple through subtle changes that allowed the laws to continue. This effectively reinvented the temple faith for Jews.

Eusebius

Eusebius, the early fourth century bishop of Caesarea, usefully discussed the still uncanonized writings for the Christian Sequel:

> At this point it may be appropriate to list the New Testament Writings already referred to. The holy quartet of the Gospels are first, followed by the Acts of the Apostle. Next are Paul's epistles, 1 John, and 1 Peter. The Revelation of John may be added, the arguments regarding which I shall discuss at the proper time. These are the recognized books. Those that are disputed yet known to most are the epistles called James, Jude, 2 Peter, and the so-named 2 and 3 John, the work of the Evangelist or of someone else with the same name.
> Among the spurious books are the Acts of Paul, the Shepherd [of Hermas], the Revelation of Peter, the alleged epistle of Barnabas, the so-called Teachings of the Apostles [Didache], as well as the Revelation of John, if appropriate here: some reject it, others accept is, as stated before. In addition, some have included the Gospel of the Hebrews in

A Natural History of Scripture

the list, for which those Hebrews who have accepted Christ have a special fondness. These would all be classified with the disputed books, those not canonical yet familiar to most church writers, which I have listed separately in order to distinguish them for those writings that are true, genuine, and accepted in the tradition of the church.

Writings published by heretics under the names of the apostles, such as the Gospels of Peter, Thomas, Matthias, and others, or the Acts of Andrew, John, and other apostles have never been cited by any in the succession of church writers. The type of phraseology used contrasts with apostolic style, and the opinions and thrusts of their contents are so dissonant from true orthodoxy that they show themselves to be forgeries of heretics. Accordingly, they ought not be reckoned even among the spurious books but discarded as impious and absurd.[79]

The Byzantine Era

Diocletian

Jews and Christians alike chose to refrain from Rome's pagan religion. Jews had long been exempt from participation, due to their monotheistic heritage, but Christians lost that exemption when the church became distinct from the synagogue. Christianity was considered a new religion and sporadic persecution of Christians grew until the Roman emperor Diocletian in AD 303 "ordered the destruction of all Christian churches and texts."[80]

In AD 305 Diocletian abdicated the throne and his innovative reorganization effort of naming four rulers over different regions of the Roman Empire began to crumble. Maximian settled into Rome and tried to reclaim the throne, but a young Constantine had the same idea. Their armies met at Marseilles in AD 310 and Constantine killed Maximian.

Constantine

Maximian's son Maxentius now fortified his army in Rome and prepared for battle with Constantine. In AD 312 Constantine and his troops approached Rome and camped near the Milvian Bridge over the Tiber. That night Constantine saw a cross in the sky and the words 'In This Sign, Conquer.' Fortified by this vision, Constantine's troops went the next day into battle and won, with Constantine himself throwing Maxentius off the bridge where he drowned in the Tiber.

Constantine was converted to Christianity right then and there, moved into Rome and established himself as Emperor of the West. In AD 313 Constantine issued the Edict of Milan, which made Christianity a legally recognized form of worship. In AD 324 Constantine defeated his last rival, Licinius, Emperor of the East, and finally imposed sole control over the entire empire. As Christianity replaced paganism, factions inside Christianity threatened to split it.

A Natural History of Scripture

The Council of Nicaea

Fierce theological battles raged throughout the Roman Empire over the question of how Jesus was divine. This had long been the dividing point for Jews, but now Christians were becoming divided about this issue. Enjoying his new political unity, Constantine convened a council in Nicaea in AD 325 to bring about religious unity. This gathering of bishops hammered out the beginnings of what became The Nicene Creed and those who disagreed with it were excommunicated.

While in Nicaea, Constantine made side trips to the ancient Greek city of Byzantium to oversee construction of his new city. Constantinople was to be the capital of his newly unified empire, built over the old city, and it would be an exclusively Christian place. In AD 330, Constantinople indeed became the capital of the Roman Empire, Christianity began a program of expansion, and Judaism came under attack. This was the birth of the Byzantine Era.

The Vulgate and the Apocrypha

Have you ever noticed that some Bibles include a collection of writings called the Apocrypha? Apocrypha means 'things that are hidden' because Jerome left these books out of his Latin translation of the Hebrew Scriptures, known as the Vulgate. Jerome was commissioned in AD 383 by Pope Damasus to update the scriptures by producing an authoritative Latin Bible. He translated from the Greek Septuagint (which included the Apocrypha), but removed them because the Hebrew canon had already been determined and these books were never

A Natural History of Scripture

part of the Hebrew Scriptures. These books were written from about 400 BC to 250 BC.

Augustine was successful a couple of centuries later in including the Apocrypha as part of the full Hebrew/Christian Bible. About a thousand years later they were removed again by Martin Luther when he translated the Bible into German during the Protestant Reformation. The Catholic Church has never removed the Apocrypha and has accepted most of its books as part of the Christian canon. Today there is a growing acceptance among Protestants to recognize the Apocrypha as intertestamental writings.

This collection of books had only two things in common: 1) they were written after the last of the prophets—Malachi, and 2) some were written in Hebrew while other books were written in Greek (this common bond separates it from the Hebrew canon which was all written in Hebrew [or Aramaic] and the Christian canon which was all written in Greek).

The titles of the Apocryphal books can be found in the chart on the next page.[81]

A Natural History of Scripture

The Apocrypha

> 1 Esdras
>
> 2 Esdras
>
> Tobit
>
> Judith
>
> The Additions to the Book of Esther
>
> The Wisdom of Solomon
>
> Ecclesiasticus
>
> Baruch
>
> A Letter of Jeremiah
>
> The Prayer of Azariah and the Song of the Three
>
> Susanna
>
> Bel and the Dragon
>
> The Prayer of Manasseh
>
> 1 Maccabees
>
> 2 Maccabees

Figure 10

A Natural History of Scripture

Canonization of the Christian Sequel

The origin and formation of the Christian canon went through a process similar to that of the Hebrew canon, but in a decidedly shorter amount of time. There was still an oral stage, followed by a writing stage, followed by an editing stage, followed by the selection process of canonization. The two canons are also similar in that they each developed in a tripartite style. While the Hebrew canon had the Law, the Prophets, and the Writings, the Christian canon ended up with the Gospels, Paul's Epistles, and the Letters.

There seems to have been no conscious movement in the early days of Christianity to produce a new collection of sacred books. The Greek translation of the Hebrew Scriptures, known as the Septuagint, supplied sufficient material to make Christians happy, when interpreted from the perspective of Jesus. The two historical forces that facilitated the canonization of the Christian Sequel were: 1) Marcionism, which sought to make the canon too small, and 2) Gnosticism, which tried to make the canon too large.

In his festal letter of Easter AD 367, Athansius, bishop of Alexandria, listed the twenty-seven books that now make up our canon. Jerome and Augustine listed the same twenty-seven books but recognized that all the churches had not accepted some of the books. The Third Council of Carthage (AD 397) resolved that only canonical writings should be recognized as divine Scriptures, and for all practical purposes it can be said that the canonization process concluded with the Council of Chalcedon (AD 451).

A Natural History of Scripture

Other Important People and Events

A Sack of Rome

As Constantinople increased in power, Rome decreased. The western part of the Roman Empire grew poorer because as "taxes went up, more people left the towns and sought to live self-sufficiently in the country to avoid them. Less money meant a poorer army, and that meant more reliance on barbarian mercenaries—which cost still more money."[82] In AD 410 Rome itself was sacked by the Visigoths, signifying the beginning of the end of the Roman Empire.

Augustine

The sack of Rome was such a shock that St. Augustine wrote a book to explain how God fit into the picture. In AD 427 he published *The City of God*, which claimed the disaster in the new Christian Empire came from immorality. Those who lived in the flesh were part of the City of Man and the inevitable result would be war, such as what had happened in Rome. Those who lived in the spirit were part of the City of God and the inevitable result would be love.

Another issue Augustine dealt with in his book was the Jews. The growing Christian attitude toward the Jews was a deadly enmity, but Augustine reversed the tradition by suggesting the Jews be spared. He took the position that the Jews had a place in God's plan of salvation by way of prophecy. To maintain Judaism was to maintain their prophetic heritage which foretold Christ, but Augustine's final suggestion was to disperse them. In AD 429 the emperor followed up on this idea and abolished Jewish rule in Israel. This ultimately led to the development of Jewish academies in Babylonia, which would pursue a self-understanding independent of Christianity through furthering the work of the Mishna.

The Fall of Rome to the Visigoths

The Visigoths continued to plunder through the Latin West and eventually arrived in France. Another group of barbarians, the Vandals, had overrun Spain and now the two groups were near one another. The emperor enlisted the Visigoths to battle the Vandals, and they managed to push them to the southern tip of Spain. The Vandals crossed the Straits of Gibraltar and settled in Carthage in North Africa. In AD 455 the Vandals crossed the Mediterranean and Rome was once again sacked. In AD 476 the last western emperor was killed, the Roman Empire ceased, and Constantinople became the seat of the Byzantine era.

Justinian

In AD 527 Justinian became emperor in Constantinople and passionately pursued Christian unity. He saw priests and the emperor as the two greatest gifts from God and they were to work symbiotically: "While Christian priests prayed for the welfare of the emperor, the emperor guaranteed the support, dignity, and order of the priesthood in the world."[83] In AD 529

A Natural History of Scripture

Justinian closed the non-Christian philosophical schools in Athens and soon thereafter Benedict of Nursia established a rule at his monastery of Monte Cassino in Italy. The Rule of St. Benedict created sacred space and time so as to experience Augustine's heavenly City of God here on earth.

In AD 532 Justinian sponsored the construction of a great church in Constantinople. Completed in AD 537 Saint Sophia became the meeting point of heaven and earth. The unity Justinian desired did not materialize because he rejected the Council of Chalcedon's doctrine of the dual nature of Jesus as fully human and fully divine. Meanwhile, in the West, unity was redeveloped in Rome by the belief in an unbroken apostolic succession dating back to Saint Peter.

Muhammad

Muhammad was born in AD 570 in Arabia at Mecca. His father died before he was born, his mother died when he was six, and he was raised by his uncle. Little is known about his childhood, and when he was 25 he married a wealthy 40 year-old widow. Economic security allowed him more time to visit a popular cave outside Mecca where he would go for a month each year.

It was in the cave that Muhammad began to contemplate the fate of his fellow Arabs. A burgeoning trade in Mecca had brought tremendous success, but Muhammad noticed a diminishing interest in old tribal values. Capitalism was creating a virtual worship of money and individualism was replacing community. Muhammad had been influenced by

A Natural History of Scripture

Judaism and Christianity and believed the Arabs needed a prophet and text of their own to solve their problems.

The Qur'an

In the year 610 Muhammad received a vision while at the cave. The angel Gabriel revealed it (Qur'an 2:97), and these communications continued until 622. These recitations provided the birth of the Qur'an, which were written down by his followers after his death. The last ten years of Muhammad's life was spent establishing the Islamic faith. The word 'Islam' means submission and the Muslim faith is one that calls all people to submit to the one God.

Most Meccans rejected Muhammad's message and he lived a difficult life of persecution after the communications began. By 615 some of his followers fled the country and in 619 Muhammad's wife and uncle died. At this time Muhammad was said to have been taken by Gabriel to Jerusalem where he ascended to heaven from what has become the Dome of the Rock. Upon return to Mecca he preached even more fervently to become a Muslim.

As the leaders of Mecca became angrier, Muhammad sent most of his followers to what became known as Medina, or the City of the Prophet. On July 16, 622 Muhammad himself fled to Medina and this date became the beginning of the Islamic calendar. Muhammad considered Abraham the model Muslim because of his faithful surrender to Allah, the one God. In 630 Muhammad made a pilgrimage to Mecca which established the rites of *hajj* or pilgrimage. On June 8, 632 Muhammad died and was buried in Medina.

A Natural History of Scripture

The Islamic faith provided a path to heaven and the avoidance of hell. The world was seen as consisting of those who followed Allah, the Qur'an, and the traditions of Muhammad, and those who needed to be brought to submission under Islam. The crescent moon became their symbol, representing their mission of spreading Islam from Mecca to the moon.

The Qur'an said that it was a revelation from God as were "the Torah and the Gospel" (Qur'an 3:3). It also acknowledged that the Torah and Gospel were given to Moses and Jesus respectively (Qur'an 2:87). It warned that infidels, those who did not submit to the will of the one God, would not be punished until they had received a messenger (Qur'an 17:15). Of course Muhammad was seen as the final messenger, so infidels beware. The punishment was a *jihad*, which simply meant struggle, but unbelievers could be exposed to total war (Qur'an 9:5).

What was at stake was nothing less than a sacred history. Just as Christianity appropriated the sacred history of Judaism, so Islam appropriated the sacred history of Christianity. Christianity saw itself as the fulfillment of Judaism through Jesus as the Messiah. Islam saw itself as the fulfillment of Christianity through correcting its polytheistic sounding doctrine of Trinity. Jesus was seen as a prophet, like Moses and Muhammad, not the Son of God. Correcting the gospel story of crucifixion, the Qur'an had Jesus experience the divine intervention of direct ascension to heaven. The Jews "neither killed nor crucified him, though it so appeared to them" (Qur'an 4:157).

A Natural History of Scripture

The Talmuddim

The codification of the oral law into the Mishnah some four hundred years earlier proved to be extremely useful. Academies of learning sprang up in Babylonia and Palestine and the Mishnah could then be studied and updated separately in each locale. The Palestinian academies were located in Tiberias, Caesarea and Sepphoris and the Babylonian academies were located in Sura and Pumbedita. The scholars who discussed the Mishnah were known as the *amoraim* and their material is known as the Gemara, which means completion.

The Talmuddim, plural for Talmud, represented the compilations of Mishnah with its associated Gemara in the separate communities. This gave rabbinic Judaism a distinct identity completely separate from Christianity. Christians appreciated the Mosaic Law, but the Mishnaic law was updated strictly for the Jews. The resulting Talmuddim provided a uniquely Jewish faith and the Babylonian Talmud ultimately became the most authoritative.

Palestinian Talmud

By the end of the fourth century, the *amoraim* of Palestine had gathered together the past two hundred years of discussions about the Mishnah. Their Gemara represented responses to only the first four of six 'orders' of the Mishnah. Nothing is known as to how the Palestinian Talmud was put together nor why the last two orders of the Mishna are missing. Work was halted in the 420s when the Roman Emperor ended Jewish rule in Israel.

Babylonian Talmud

By the end of the sixth century, the *amoraim* of Babylon had gathered together the past four hundred years of discussions about the Mishnah. Their Gemara covered a little less of the Mishnah than their Palestinian counterpart, but it was "nearly four times as long, with approximately two-and-a-half million words."[84] It is not known how much of an influence the Palestinian Talmud may have had on the Babylonian Talmud, but it certainly reflected daily Jewish life in 4th/5th century Babylon.

The Fall of Jerusalem to the Arabs

After the death of Muhammad, Muslim leadership was passed on to men with the title Caliph, meaning successor. At this point the Arab nation swept through North Africa, Western Asia and Europe. Although the Caliphs provided the leadership, not all of the Arabs were converted to Islam. They took Damascus in 635, all of Syria in 636, then after a two year siege they captured Jerusalem.

Islam's beginning was violent, but the Qur'an taught harmony. The word "*islam* derives from the same root as *salam* ('peace'),"[85] but the surrender to God that would bring peace became understood as a mission to save the world.

A Natural History of Scripture

The endless struggle of *jihad* became a task of restoration for the whole world to return to the original perfection intended by God. Jerusalem provided a place to experience that original perfection, since it was the home of the other two monotheistic religions. They built a mosque on the Temple Mount, which is where the al-Aqsa Mosque still stands today.

Dome of the Rock

In 688 work began on the Dome of the Rock in Jerusalem, which was a shrine rather than a Mosque. This is where tradition says Muhammad ascended to heaven before returning to Mecca. This is where tradition also says Abraham brought his son Isaac for sacrifice as a test of submission. The only thing missing at this site was Christianity, so an inscription over the arches of the inner arcade warned about the Christian problems that Islam corrected: "The Christ Jesus, son of Mary, was but God's apostle—[the fulfillment of] His promise which he had conveyed unto Mary—and a soul created by Him. Believe then in God and his apostle and do not say '[God] is a trinity.' Desist [from this assertion] for your own good. God is but One God: utterly remote is He in his glory from having a son" (Qur'an 4:171, 172; 10:34-37).

Karaism

The Karaites were an anti-rabbinic sect that started in the eighth century as a movement against Mishnaic law. Their stance was that Mosaic law represented the true religion and later rabbinic interpretations in the Mishnah and the Talmud represented unnecessary changes. They had a literalistic interpretation of Torah, which proved to be much more demanding than the Judaism of the time.

Karaism grew for a couple of centuries then stabilized, and even today there are "approximately ten thousand Karaites, most of whom live in Israel."[86] Karaism flourished initially in the Islamic Empire and one of their many scholarly contributions was the translation of the Hebrew Scriptures into Arabic. Karaites were generally treated as Jews by their host nations but the Nazis of the twentieth century considered them not to be of Jewish stock. Today they are not allowed to intermarry with Jews.

Charlemagne

Constantinople served as a military barrier for the development of Christianity in Europe. As Christian armies fought and won battles in Constantinople against marauding invaders, Europe was experiencing a rapid spread of Christianity. From about AD 750 there was a cooperative spirit "between the Frankish rulers and bishops of Rome."[87] With so much trouble in the Mediterranean, Rome quit looking for help from the east (Constantinople) and focused attention on the north, over the Alps.

By AD 768 Charlemagne was the king of the Franks, and he continued to strengthen relationships with Rome. In the summer of 800, Charlemagne traveled to Rome to vindicate Pope Leo III from charges of corruption. Unable to return over

A Natural History of Scripture

the Alps because of bad weather, he remained in Rome. On Christmas Day, Charlemagne attended services at St. Peter's and Pope Leo III crowned him as the new Roman Emperor. This monumental act was particularly shocking to Irene who was the Roman Empress living in Constantinople.

Spanish Jewry

Spain had a series of tolerant Muslim leaders in the tenth century and many Jews held government positions while Judaism flourished. One of the great contributions from this era was a commentary on the Torah by Abraham ibn Ezra. Although life generally went well for the Jews in Spain through the twelfth century, things abruptly came to an end. A tyrannical Muslim leader invaded from North Africa and gave the Jews three choices: conversion to Islam, exile, or death.

Standardizing the Hebrew Text

The text of the Hebrew Scriptures became almost completely standardized between AD 70 and AD 135. This process attempted to resolve differences in three manuscript traditions: 1) Hebrew scrolls written in Babylon during the exile in the sixth century BC, 2) Hebrew scrolls translated into Greek (the Septuagint) in Egypt in the third century BC, and 3) Hebrew scrolls written in Palestine before the Babylonian exile.

The problem is that none of the original scrolls of the three manuscript traditions exist. We do have later copies of the Septuagint, but they are suspect as a source for the basic

A Natural History of Scripture

Hebrew text because they are a translation. It wasn't until the tenth century that the Hebrew text received vowels, spaces, and punctuation. This was produced by a group of scholars known as Masoretes (meaning tradition), working in Tiberias, on the shore of the Sea of Galilee.

The result was the Masoretic Text (from the Masoretes), which was the culmination of 500 years of work. Their effort is still used "as the basis for an edition of the Hebrew Bible"[88] in Hebrew. The English version of the Hebrew Bible is called the *TANAKH*, an acronym for Torah, Nevi'im, Kethuvim, which was "made directly from the traditional Hebrew text into the idiom of modern English."[89]

The oldest copy of the Masoretic Text (MT) dates to the early part of the tenth century. It is known as the Aleppo Codex. "Formerly housed in the Aleppo synagogue (it is now in Jerusalem), the Aleppo Codex was damaged during the riots there in 1948."[90] Because the Aleppo Codex was unavailable, modern scholars relied mostly on the Leningrad Codex. Dating to about 1009, the Leningrad Codex is housed in the state library of St. Petersburg and is the oldest complete copy of the MT that has survived the centuries.

Nothing is known of "the wanderings of the Leningrad Codex until the notation in its colophon citing the bill of sale presumably in Damascus in 1489. The trail vanishes again until Abraham Firkovich turned up with it in the 1840's."[91] The value of the Masorah preserved in this manuscript cannot be overestimated. It is enough to say that "the Masorah to Genesis alone includes 2,570 notes, [and] the Masorah to the whole Bible [contains] about sixty thousand notes."[92]

A Natural History of Scripture

Rashi

Rashi is an acronym for Rabbi Shlomo ben Isaac who wrote an invaluable commentary on the Talmud. In his work he clarified difficult Aramaic words and succinctly explained the confusing logic of the Talmud. He also wrote a commentary on the Torah where he explained words at both literal and symbolic levels. His work was so important that it became the first book printed in Hebrew, even before the Torah made it to print.

The Great Schism

The events that transpired in Constantinople in 1054 were simply the culmination of centuries of troubles between the eastern and western parts of the Roman Empire. Things started coming to a head in 1046 when Henry III came to Rome to be crowned as emperor. When Pope Leo IX took office, he worked in harmony with Henry III to enact reform. The most important thing they did was to equip the position of pope with independent authority over the church.

Of course the problem was the continued strife between East and West. In the midst of their troubles, southern Italy incurred an invasion that threatened the Byzantine Empire. Constantine IX was the Eastern Emperor and Michael Cerularius was the Eastern Patriarch, and they discussed conditional help for their western neighbors. The condition called for the pope to regain control of the few Greek churches in Italy, and for the patriarch to regain control of the few Latin churches in Constantinople. The Latin churches in

A Natural History of Scripture

Constantinope refused to follow the demands of Cerularius, who responded by shutting them down.

Things got worse in 1053 when invaders captured Pope Leo. With the Byzantine Empire in jeopardy, compromise was offered, to which the west demanded full authority over the church. They claimed that Rome had succession back to Peter and that they would listen to no one. Cerularius responded by excommunicating the Roman authorities in 1054. This gave birth to the Great Schism which became the Catholic churches in the west and the Orthodox churches in the east.

The Crusades

In 1095 the Eastern Emperor became concerned about the spread of Muslim Turks. He asked for help from Pope Urban II who showed interest in healing the schism by helping the Byzantine Empire and the Orthodox Church. He also saw that this could be attached to an agenda of rescuing the Holy Land from the Muslims. Pope Urban rallied interest in his plan by preaching a sermon that God willed the rescue of the Holy Land from Islam.

The First Crusade had terrible consequences, because although the objective was conversion the practice became murder. As the Christian armies marched toward the Holy Land, they wore the cross and saw their task as a holy war. The intention was to free the Holy Land from infidels and the Pope promised eternal life and the status of martyr to anyone who died. In 1099 the crusaders captured Jerusalem after a bloody expedition of indiscriminate slaughter of Jews, Arab Christians and Muslims.

A Natural History of Scripture

Hailed as a sweeping victory, the First Crusade ultimately gave birth to the Second Crusade. Edessa was a "key city in the defenses of the Crusader's kingdom"[93] and it fell to the Turks in 1144. Inspiration for a crusade this time came from Bernard of Clairvaux in 1146. Lasting from 1147—1149, the Second Crusade was a failure. It began with a massacre of Jews and ended in disaster as the crusaders lost their attempt to take Damascus.

In 1187 the great Muslim soldier Saladin reconquered Jerusalem for Islam. This launched the Third Crusade (1189—1192) led by the Holy Roman Emperor Frederick Barbarossa, King Philip Augustus of France, and King Richard the Lionhearted of England. The Emperor died in Asia Minor, the kings quarreled, and their only success was the recapture of Acre in Palestine. Saladin offered some compromise by allowing pilgrims access to the Holy Sepulchre.

The original vision of freeing the Holy Land from Islam would not be compromised and The Fourth Crusade lasted from 1202—1204. Pope Innocent III wanted to crush Saladin, and his chief support came from Egypt. The Crusaders needed ships to cross the Mediterranean to Egypt, so they turned to the people of Venice. The Venetians focused the expedition on Constantinople for political reasons and in 1204 the Crusaders stormed Constantinople and set up a Latin Empire.

Maimonides

Rabbi Moses ben Maimon was known as Maimonides. His major contribution to Judaism was the *Mishneh Torah*, meaning second law, which was a systematic code of all Jewish law. This provided a shortcut to the expansive and difficult Talmud, which in turn caused controversy with traditional Jews who were concerned that his book would lead to a lack of study of the Talmud.

The Zohar

The *Zohar*, meaning Divine Splendor, was the most influential book of the Jewish mystical tradition, known as Kabbalah. Authored by Rabbi Moses de Leon in the thirteenth century, the story focused on a second century Rabbi. Written in five volumes of "mixed Hebrew and Aramaic biblical commentaries, fables, anecdotes, and biographical portraits,"[94] it was ultimately a commentary on the Torah in the form of a mystical novel. The Torah served as a springboard to the mystical stories about Rabbi Shim'on wandering through Galilee and exchanging insights with his companions.

Thomas Aquinas

Influenced by the philosophical work of Maimonides, Thomas Aquinas wrote *Summa Theologiae*, his masterful compendium of Christian belief. He also wrote *Summa Contra Gentiles*, his complete summary of the Christian faith. The latter was designed to help Christians convert unbelievers, particularly Jews. Ever since Augustine, the Christian community took a tolerant stance toward the Jews because they were believed to be ignorant of the truth that Jesus was the Messiah.

A Natural History of Scripture

After Aquinas published his *Summa Contra Gentiles*, Christians were shocked to find very few Jewish converts. This led to a new understanding that the Jews were not ignorant, they were defiant, and this led to fears and rumors against the Jews. Instead of protected as bearers of the Hebrew Scriptures, as Augustine called the Jews, they were now despised as bearers of the religion Jesus set himself against. The Talmud was identified as the source of Jewish defiance and was declared a work of heresy. This was the beginning of European intolerance toward Jews.

The Renaissance

There was a sense of unsettledness in Europe at this time, which produced a desire to learn in new ways. The direction the Renaissance took was to find freshness in ancient texts. Intellectuals turned to Latin, Greek, pagan and Christian sources "before Protestants deployed the authority of another ancient text, the Bible, as a justification for rejecting traditional Catholic deference to the papacy."[95]

Humanism

Petrarch (1304—1374) was an Italian poet who turned to classical Latin texts for inspiration. Rejecting the Greek philosophy of Aristotle, Petrarch turned to the philosophy of Cicero and the poetry of Ovid and Virgil. For his Christian humanism, he turned to the introspective self-examination of Augustine's *Confessions*. Petrarch read Augustine for spiritual guidance and came to the conclusion that the human self was of supreme value.

Marsilio Ficino (1433—1499) was an Italian scholar who turned to classical Greet texts for inspiration. Particularly revering the works of Plato, Ficino found that the highest ideals could be found within the human soul where even God resided. Believing in the unity of the soul with God, Ficino found that all ancient wisdom was worthy, including the works of the Persian Zoroaster, the Greek Orpheus, and the Egyptian Trismegistus. Later Christian humanism also embraced Muslim and Jewish wisdom for supporting the central importance of the human self.

Psychology

Although the modern term 'psychology' was never used, Renaissance thinkers also developed a scientific approach to the soul. They understood human psychology to be composed of three souls—"the vegetative soul, the sensitive soul, and the intellective soul."[96] The vegetative soul animated the physical body, the sensitive soul engaged voluntary and involuntary motion, emotion, and the external senses, and the intellective soul received information from the senses and transformed the data into rational concepts.

Christian psychologists thought of the sensitive soul as the spirit and developed their spirituality through imagination. They meditated on images to inspire the spirit by visualizing the signs and symbols of various planets and constellations. The hoped for result was to have the heavenly influences nurture the human spirit. This practical psychology that sought

A Natural History of Scripture

to develop the body and the soul also used music to inspire the spirit.

The Fall of Constantinople to the Turks

After nearly twelve centuries of existence, the Byzantine Empire abruptly came to a close. Constantinople had long stood as a bulwark against the Muslims, but in 1453 it fell to the Turks. The Turkish ruler Muhammad II celebrated with a thanksgiving service in the grand Saint Sophia church in Constantinople and turned the city into the capital of his Empire. Saint Sophia was turned into a mosque and later the city became the seat of the Muslim faith.

A Natural History of Scripture

Chapter 8
Publishers: Elements of Microevolution

Prenatal Stage: Storytellers	Infant Stage: Writers		Adolescent Stage: Editors			Adult Stage: Standardizers	
Oral History	Written History	Pro-phets	Priests	Trans-lators	Evan-gelists	Politi-cians	Pub-lishers

2000 BC   950 BC   750 BC 586 BC   332 BC   63 BC   AD 144   AD 1454   NOW

In a sense, printing is almost as old as writing, for the act of writing is a sort of printing. You conceive of a symbol from the store in your brain and turn out copies with pen, ink and paper.[97]

Publishers continue to pursue a standardization of the biblical text. Since the text will never reach perfection, the canonization process will gradually reopen. Since the theory of evolution says that diversity is the real story, new interest in the diverse stories of the Apocrypha and the Qur'an will evolve toward inclusion in the canon.

A Natural History of Scripture

The Printing Press

What dramatic changes the computer did for the last century, the printing press did for the fifteenth century. Right in the midst of the new learning of the Renaissance, came the vehicle needed to quickly spread these ideas all over Europe. Sometime in the mid 1450s, Johann Gutenberg invented the printing press and life would never be the same again. Not only was the Bible his first major work, but more importantly he was "a prophet of newer worlds where machines would do the work of scribes, where the printing press would displace the scriptorium, and knowledge would be diffused to countless unseen communities."[98]

The Spanish Inquisition

A twist on the concept of the Crusades produced the Spanish Inquisition. Rather than trying to convert heretics, the Inquisition sought to purify the Christian faith. Of particular concern to the priests were converted Jews, who would be brought before the Inquisition if they were suspected of secretly practicing Judaism. If they were either convicted or confessed, they would be tortured in an effort to force a confession to the truth of Christianity. Those who wouldn't concede were burned alive.

On July 30, 1492 the entire Jewish population of about 200,000 was expelled from Spain. This was a result of the Spanish Inquisition, as an effort to keep the Jewish converts loyal to Christianity. The Spanish Jews "who ended up in Turkey, North Africa, Italy, and elsewhere throughout Europe

A Natural History of Scripture

and the Arab world, were known as Sephardim—*Sefarad* being the Hebrew name for Spain."[99] All other Jews whose families came from Europe were known as Ashkenazim—*Ashkenaz* being the Hebrew name for Germany.

Joseph Karo

Although Maimonides had produced a systematic code of all Jewish law, it only contained the legal rulings of the Sephardic Jews. Since the expulsion of the Jews from Spain, a new code was needed to include the developing traditions of the Ashkenazic Jews. Rabbi Joseph Karo ended up compiling a code that listed the different customs and laws of both communities and his work is known as the *Shulkhan Arukh*. This exhaustive compilation still stands as the standard legal code of Judaism.

Erasmus' Edition of the Greek New Testament

Desiderius Erasmus was born in about 1466, ordained as a priest in 1492, and became a champion of humanism. He loved the classics and fiercely defended learning from pagan authors like Virgil. Citing the example that the church had not abandoned the Hebrew Scriptures even though it was full of laws that Christians did not follow, he claimed that "the Church should not abandon the classics because they celebrated pagan gods."[100] As Erasmus immersed himself in translating ancient texts, it crossed his mind that the Holy Scriptures were Jerome's translation into Latin. In 1516 he published a Greek

A Natural History of Scripture

edition of the New Testament, and thanks to the printing press, it opened the door for the Protestant Reformation.

Martin Luther's Ninety-Five Theses

Martin Luther was born in 1483, ordained as a priest in 1507, and became a champion of defiance against the Catholic Church. His ire was roused in 1517 by the Catholic practice of selling forgiveness and proceeded to put together his Ninety-Five Theses against the Catholic Church. The printing press made his ideas known in a much quicker time to a much greater audience. Luther believed that it was not the church that could change people, it was the gospel. Claiming authority of scripture alone, "Luther found that salvation was an undeserved gift of divine grace received through faith. The principles *sola scriptura, sola gratia, sola fides*—only according to scripture, by grace, through faith—were regarded by Luther and his followers as marking the new divide between Protestants and Catholics in European Christianity."[101]

The Diet of Worms

In April of 1521, Luther was summoned to the modest city of Worms, Germany to recant his positions before the imperial diet (formal assembly). He said that he would if anyone there could indicate where the Bible proved him wrong. His protest against any other authority than scripture gave birth to the Protestant Reformation. If the Bible was going to be useful to the people as a means of authority, he knew that it needed to be accessible in their language. In 1522 Martin Luther published a German translation of Erasmus' Greek Edition of the New Testament, which came to be called the Reformation Bible.

Part of what Luther hoped to accomplish with his reformation was something the Catholic Church failed to do: convert Jews to Christianity. After twenty years of Protestant failure, Martin Luther turned sour and produced one of the most anti-Semitic writings since Muhammad's thoughts in the Qur'an. In his *Concerning the Jews and Their Lies*, he outlined eight proposals for dealing with the Jews:

1. Burn all synagogues.
2. Destroy all Jewish homes.
3. Confiscate all Jewish holy books.
4. Forbid rabbis to teach, on pain of death.
5. Forbid Jews to travel.
6. Confiscate Jewish property.
7. Force Jews to do physical labor.
8. [And, in case the preceding restrictions proved insufficient] Expel all the Jews.[102]

Zwingli's War Against Idols

Huldreich Zwingli was born in 1484 in Switzerland and became a champion of the Reformed Churches. Switzerland was unique at that time because it was essentially independent from the Holy Roman Empire, which led to an

A Natural History of Scripture

easier revolt against the Catholic Church than the Protestants experienced. In 1519 Zwingli became a priest in Zurich and in 1520 he rejected financial support from the Pope. Receiving moral support from the civil rulers, Zwingli led the revolt by denouncing any religious practice that was not warranted in the scriptures.

In 1522 Zwingli launched a campaign to remove all religious images from the churches in Zurich. The city council agreed and through official edict all images other than the cross were removed. Zwingli's point was that the images promoted idol worship and true religion needed to focus on the spiritual God. A major difference between the Swiss reformers and the German reformers developed over the Eucharist. Zwingli saw communion as a spiritual thing and Luther saw it as a physical thing. Luther eased the war against idols while Zwingli increased it. Zwingli was killed in 1531 fighting a military battle between Swiss Catholics and Protestants.

Tyndale's English Translation

As the Reformation spread, the importance of having the Bible translated into native languages became apparent. William Tyndale (AD 1494—AD 1536) became the pioneer for an English translation. Born in England and schooled at Oxford, Tyndale found himself at odds with Oxford over the issue of translation. Tyndale had Luther's heart for making the scriptures accessible to the people, but Oxford held an academic commitment to the Latin language and saw no need to translate the Vulgate.

A Natural History of Scripture

Tyndale moved to London in hopes of translating the New Testament into English, but his efforts were rejected. He settled into Cologne, Germany in 1524 and completed his task the following year. Just after the printing process began, the printing house was raided. Tyndale escaped with his original translation and set up shop again in Worms. This time he went undetected and the first English translation of the New Testament was printed in 1526. It was this edition that was "smuggled into England and created irreversible pressure for an English Bible."[103]

When translating from one language to another, there is often no word that properly expresses the original. Tyndale introduced many new words into the English language by creating words to accommodate biblical ideas. He was the one who made up the word "Jehovah" for God's name by combining a Latin transliteration of the tetragrammaton, *jhvh*, with the vowels from the Hebrew word for Lord, *adonai*. In trying to translate the word for the Jewish festival of *Pesah*, he came up with the word "Passover." In 1536 Tyndale was arrested for heresy and strangled to death.

Founding of the Jesuits

Ignatius Loyola was a solider who was wounded in battle. During convalescence he read devotional literature about the life of Christ which affected him so much that he decided to enter the priesthood. He developed a depth of spirituality that transformed him deeper into the Catholic Church, which drew a following of people who wanted to pledge themselves to missionary service. In response to Loyola's request, the Pope established a new religious order and called it the Society of Jesus. The founding of the Jesuits proved to be a major contribution to the Catholic Counter-Reformation.

Calvin's Protestant Order

John Calvin (1509—1564) was living in Paris as a lawyer when he became sympathetic to the ideas of the Reformation. Fearing for his safety he fled to the Swiss city of Basel where he wrote his influential book *The Institutes of the Christian Religion*. He then decided to settle in Strasbourg, but as he passed through Geneva he was recognized as the author of the *Institutes* and asked to stay and help them organize their Reformation.

He touched a political hot point about a Genevan ally and lost the battle, being thrown out of Geneva in 1538. He then went on to Strasbourg and lived there from 1538-1541. Instability ensued in Geneva and the city council reluctantly decided to ask Calvin back rather than continue in chaos. John Calvin returned to Geneva in 1541 and spent the remaining twenty-three years of his life bringing Protestant order and making Geneva the model city of the Reformed movement.

Closing of the Christian Sequel

In a reaction to the Protestant Reformation, the Catholics called together the Council of Trent to standardize Catholic beliefs. The Council met in three sessions (1545-47, 1551-52, 1562—63) where they confirmed such ideas as the Latin Vulgate was to be used as the official Scripture of the church rather than translations into any other languages. These types of stances seemed to create irreconcilable differences between the Protestants and the Catholics.

The most important challenge to the canon of the New Testament came from Martin Luther in the early sixteenth century. He had theological problems with Hebrews, James, Jude, and Revelation, and "placed these four books at the end of his German translation of the NT, though he did not remove them from the Bible."[104] At its fourth session in April 1546, the Council of Trent for the first time in Christianity pronounced the twenty-seven books of the New Testament as a closed canon.

King James' Authorized Version of the Bible

Translating the Bible into any vernacular was a highly political act, because it continued to show defiance to the Catholic Church. Translating the Bible into English had the added element of proclaiming dignity for the increasingly popular status of England. Queen Elizabeth propelled England to global greatness, and when she died in 1603 the naming of her successor was critical. With no obvious choice, the task fell upon an outsider—James, the son of Mary Queen of Scots.

King James inherited the Geneva Bible as the Bible of choice of English Protestants, but he disliked it because it contained politically oriented annotations that could undermine his authority. In 1604 King James convened the Hampton Court Conference to reform problems within the church. His

A Natural History of Scripture

first comment was that he, "as king, would have a decisive role in the affairs of the church."[105] He knew that he did not want to authorize the Geneva Bible, so when a new Bible translation was proposed, he was more than interested.

James directed the best scholars at Oxford and Cambridge to begin work on a new translation of the whole Bible from the original Hebrew and Greek, without annotations, for all churches to use. King James and the Archbishop of Canterbury devised and approved limiting rules for the translators to follow, which called for heavy reliance on previous English translations that agreed with their political agenda. The King James Bible was completed and published without fanfare in 1611. It took fifty years to find acceptance among the English people and another two hundred years to begin garnering accolades.

*See the next two pages
for a comparison of
old English translations.*

A Comparison of Old English Translations

Bible	Date	Text (Psalm 23:1)
Coverdale Bible	1535	The LORDE is my shepherde, I can wante nothinge.
Matthew's Bible	1537	The Lord is my shepherde, I can want nothynge.

A Natural History of Scripture

Great Bible	1539	The Lorde is my shepherde, therefore can I lack nothing.
Geneva Bible	1560	The Lorde is my shepherd, I shal not want.
Bishop's Bible	1568	God is my sheephearde, therefore I can lacke nothyng.
Douai Old Testament	1609-1610	Our Lord ruleth me, and nothing shal be wanting to me.
King James Bible	1611	The LORD is my shepheard, I shall not want.

Figure 11

Shabbetai Zevi

Palestine was still under Turkish Muslim rule at this time, so the Jews began to dream once again of the independence of their Holy Land. Into this scene stepped a thirty-nine-year-old Turkish Jew named Shabbetai Zevi. Messianic hopes were awakened because this young man had an insider's ability to deal with the Turks. Believing himself to be the Messiah, Shabbatai confronted the Turkish sultan and demanded the return of the land of Palestine to the Jews.

A Natural History of Scripture

Massive numbers of Jews the world over heard of this daring maneuver and began packing for their trip home. The event went poorly and Shabbetai was offered conversion to Islam or death. The messianic frenzy quickly subsided when it was discovered that Shabbetai took the Muslim name Mehemet Effendi.

The Enlightenment

This was a period of history that called upon new understandings from science and reason. Knowledge became a thing to be trusted and the idea of progress became fundamental. This intellectual revolution provided a whole new way of looking at God and argument would generally fail to bring anyone to belief. Many Protestants reacted by stepping away from traditional dogma and building a new faith around experience.

Benedict Spinoza

A Dutch Jew of Spanish descent grew up to become one of the first great Enlightenment thinkers. Disillusioned with his study of Talmud and Kaballah, Benedict Spinoza became a pantheist, believing that God and nature were the same thing. This doctrine earned him an excommunication from Judaism by the rabbis of Amsterdam, and he went on to become an early forerunner of both biblical criticism and atheism.

A Natural History of Scripture

Philip Jacob Spener

Pastoring as a German Lutheran in Frankfort, Philp Jacob Spener (1635-1705) sought to deepen the spiritual life of his parishioners. To accomplish this goal, he "gathered in his home a group for the cultivation of the Christian life through the discussion of the Sunday sermons, prayer, and the study of the Bible."[106] This gave birth to the movement known as Pietism, and the self-discipline he advocated was described in his book *Pia Desideria*, published in 1675.

Walli-Ullah

While the Enlightenment raged on through Europe, the Muslim world was relatively unaffected. The first Muslim to sense that the Islamic faith needed to respond to all the changes was the Indian Sufi Shah Walli-Ullah of Delhi. He felt that the Muslim world needed to unite to preserve their heritage and he pursued this by trying to reform the Sunnis and Shiis toward common ground. Walli-Ullah was suspicious of the movement toward colonialization and his son led a *jihad* against the British. His efforts proved to be too little, too late as the British took control of India in 1767.

Moses Mendelssohn

Living in Berlin, Moses Mendelssohn endured a climate of anti-Semitism. His unique charm garnered a following of distinguished Germans who sought improved attitudes toward

A Natural History of Scripture

Jews. His greatest contribution to Jewish education was a German translation of the Bible, accompanied by a Hebrew commentary. His followers were known as *maskilim* (enlightened ones), who gave up Yiddish, began writing in Hebrew, and found the Talmud to be irrelevant to their everyday life.

John and Charles Wesley

The stark rationalism of the Enlightenment gave birth to a new kind of piety. Moving from the head to the heart, followers of the Wesley brothers believed they were returning to the true Christianity of the first century Christians. While teaching at Oxford, John Wesley founded the Holy Club for undergraduates. Following a methodical discipline, its members became known as Methodists.

In 1738, John had a conversion experience in a chapel on Aldersgate Street in London. While Luther's preface to Romans was being read, John felt his heart strangely warmed. At that moment he realized that he could put his whole trust in Christ for salvation and find freedom from the burden of sin. The message of God's grace became the foundation of his ministry, and his brother Charles wrote nearly ten thousand hymns for their cause.

The French Revolution

France had been experiencing political, intellectual, and social tensions for quite awhile that led to the French

A Natural History of Scripture

Revolution of 1789, which proved to be one of those defining moments in time after which the world would never again be the same. In June a new National Assembly was formed; in July a popular uprising in Paris stormed and liberated the Bastille; in August the National Assembly declared that rights resided in individuals rather than church or state. Roman Catholicism was abandoned and church property was sold for the good of the state.

Modernity

In many ways, the French Revolution marked the birth of modernity. It represented the end of Christendom as the dominant world religion of the past fifteen hundred years. The Modern Era proved to be more tolerant of religious diversity, democracy, and freedom, and less tolerant of tradition, monarchy, and conservativism.

Reform Judaism

The Jews of Germany in the early 1800s responded to Modernity by radically altering some of their most cherished traditions. Reform Judaism held onto the idea that Judaism was a religion, but let go of the idea that Judaism was a race. They also lost interest in reclaiming the Holy Land, as that seemed more a matter of nationalism than religion. Other changes included dropping many Jewish laws (both Mosaic and Mishnaic), dropping the study of the Hebrew language, and dropping many of the Jewish rituals.

A Natural History of Scripture

Karl Marx (AD 1818 - AD 1883)

As revolution swept the land, a new voice arose, promoting even more violence in the search for equality. In 1848 a thirty-year-old Karl Marx and his friend Friedrich Engles published the *Communist Manifesto*. Giving birth to communist theory, they called for working class people to unite and overthrow society as it stood. Marx later published *Das Kapital* which "constitutes one of the most influential books of modern times. In the twentieth century nearly half of the world is organized on the basis of its teachings."[107]

Sigmund Freud (AD 1856 - AD 1939)

Atheism slowly crept into the fabric of society as an expression of religious tolerance and diversity. Sigmund Freud became one of the most influential Jews of the nineteenth and twentieth centuries, because he carved out the groundwork of psychoanalysis as a scientific rather than a religious viewpoint. The motivation for his theory was to explain the ferocity of antisemitism from an atheistic worldview, since he was an avowed atheist.

Charles Darwin (AD 1809 - AD 1882)

After studying to become a doctor and a minister, Darwin became a naturalist. In 1830 the *Principles of Geology* was published by Charles Lyell, which proved a previous theory that the earth developed naturally rather than

A Natural History of Scripture

supernaturally. The following year, Darwin set out on a five-year, round-the-world expedition to collect specimens and in 1859 he published his finding in *Origin of Species*.

Lyell had intentionally avoided the question of origins, but Darwin's theological training gave him comfort to tackle it. In 1871 Darwin applied his theory of natural selection to human beings and published *Descent of Man*, which postulated that humans descended from monkey-like creatures. Judeo-Christians were not happy. They had learned to cope with the changes brought on by the scientific revolution, but now science was meddling with history. How was the Bible going to survive an attack on its creation story?

Reinterpreting Scripture

The Bible had always been taught as history, but now science was offering an alternative understanding. Rather than dismissing scripture, some began suggesting that it simply needed reinterpreted. As the modern age began to open eyes to a new truth of scripture, people began to admit that the Bible was more than history. Rather than tearing down faith, this reinterpreting built an ever better faith. The Bible was beginning to be seen for what it was—sacred stories full of laws, prophecies, poems, wisdom, parables, letters, and yes, even history.

Science and religion slowly worked toward a resolution of their conflicts by realizing that truth needed context: the Bible was true about faith issues and nature was true about science issues. The unresolved problem was the fact that history was both a faith issue and a science issue.

A Natural History of Scripture

Early Responses

The Greek New Testament

In an effort to let the truth of the faith speak as clearly as possible, tradition needed to be confronted. The Roman Catholics were claiming that truth was solely embodied in St. Jerome's Latin Vulgate version of the Bible, while German Protestants preferred varying forms of Luther's translation and British Protestants used the King James Version. The problem was that each of these received texts relied on later manuscripts rather than early Greek manuscripts.

The first "clear and decisive break with the *textus receptus* came with the work of Karl Lachmann (1831). His procedure in establishing the text of the Greek NT was to give no consideration to the 'received readings' (i.e., the *textus receptus)* but only to the most ancient MSS known to him."[108] This triumph over the *textus receptus* combined with striking new manuscript discoveries in the next few decades. The major advancement came in 1881 with the publication of *The Greek New Testament in the Original Greek*.

The Documentary Hypothesis

For a long time it was assumed that Moses wrote the first five books of the Hebrew scriptures, but many questions haunted this assumption. Why were there two creation stories? Why were there different names for God? Why is the sacred mountain sometimes called Sinai and at other times called Horeb? How could Moses write of his own death? The

A Natural History of Scripture

problem was that church and synagogue considered these questions heretical.

The Protestant Reformation actually brought about the first challenge to the church's traditional interpretation of scripture, then reason became a more and more acceptable tool for interpretation with the coming of the Enlightenment. Finally, the rise of biblical criticism (the reasoned critique of scripture) gave birth to what was called the Documentary Hypothesis. This is where the first five books of the Hebrew scriptures were recognized as being not by Moses but about Moses.

This theory suggests that four authors wrote at different times, and the Torah as we know it today was the work of an editor who wove the stories together during and after the exile. Julius Wellhausen gave the classical exposition to this four-source theory when he popularized the previously proposed arguments for the historical-critical study of the Old Testament. The Documentary Hyposthesis became known as the JEDP source theory as follows:

> For working purposes, the four documents were identified by alphabetic symbols. The document that was associated with the divine name Yahweh/Jehovah was called J. The document that was identified as referring to the deity as God (in Hebrew, Elohim) was called E. The third document, by far the largest, included most of the legal sections and concentrated a great deal on matters having to do with priests, and so it was called P. And the source that was found only in the book of Deuteronomy was called D.[109]

A Natural History of Scripture

The J document was believed to be written around 1000 BC from the southern kingdom of Judah. J consistently called God by his personal name, *Yahweh*, showing some sense of intimate relationship. J was also clear that sin consisted of disobedience to *Yahweh* and "was more concerned to show the effects of sin than to analyze its cause."[110]

The E document was believed to be written around 850 BC from the northern kingdom of Israel, and exclusively used the word *Elohim* when referring to God. The individual who produced the E document may have been a priest. This could have tainted his presentation of Moses as he "sought to justify the authority of the priesthood by praising its purported founder and draping him in the mantle of a miracle worker."[111]

The D document was believed to be written around 600 BC and was responsible for most of Deuteronomy. It called God by several names: *Yahweh*, *Elohim*, and *Adonai*. The author provided a theology of history, which shared his opinion that obedience to Yahweh would be beneficial and disobedience would be detrimental. The central truth he wanted to share was that "Israel's vitality and solidarity lay in a united, exclusive loyalty to Yahweh."[112]

The P document was believed to be written by priests after the exile around 500 BC. It was responsible for most of Leviticus and used the names *Elohim* and *Shaddai* when talking of God. This school of thought also produced the first creation story, which conveyed their thought that the world was created with pattern and meaning. They shared a vision of God, which produced "the omnipotent, transcendent, and benevolent God of classical theism."[113]

Once the separate sources of authorship were understood, it became obvious that an even later editor linked

A Natural History of Scripture

the sources together. It is to R (which stands for Redactor, meaning editor), "that we owe the Bible as it now lies before us."[114] In fact, the Hebrew Scriptures were literally formed by editors. These ancient people had enough respect for the separate stories they edited together, that they left inconsistencies rather than change them.

The editing of many stories into one is one of the greatest secrets to understanding the formation of the Bible.

The Balfour Declaration

The British Foreign Secretary Lord Arthur Balfour was instrumental in passing the Balfour Declaration, which favored the establishment of a homeland for the Jews in Palestine. This monumental support was particularly heartening in light of the fact that England was preparing to capture Palestine from Turkey. The transition of control of Palestine from Turkey to England set the stage for the eventual reclaiming of the Holy Land by the Jews in 1948. When that happened, it represented the first time the Holy Land was in Jewish hands in over two thousand years.

The Hebrew Bible

Even though the Hebrew Bible was thoroughly standardized by AD 1009 with the publication of the Leningrad Codex, it still

A Natural History of Scripture

was not a book available to the masses. Local synagogues bought handwritten scrolls at great price, but the Bible written in Hebrew was not a book that could be bought. In 1929, Rudolf Kittel published a critical edition of the Hebrew Bible based on the Leningrad Codex. Just as Karl Lachmann struggled to break from the *textus receptus* for the text of the Greek New Testament a century before, Kittle also battled to defend his choice of the Leningrad Codex. The Aleppo Codex was older but incomplete, so he stayed with the Leningrad Codex as the basis for his new edition of the Hebrew Bible.

The Holocaust

Christian teaching and practice found its logical conclusion in the Holocaust. Starting with the attitude of the twelfth century Crusades, Christians believed that Jews had no right to live among them without being baptized. The intent was conversion but the action was often murder. Moving to the attitude of the fifteenth century Inquisition, Christians believed that Jews had no right to live among them. The intent was expulsion but the action still was often murder. Concluding with the attitude of the twentieth century Holocaust, Christians believed that Jews had no right to live. The intent was murder and the action was called the Final Solution.

Reinterpreting God

This terrible blight on human history begged the question of God's action in history. Theologians began reinterpreting God

A Natural History of Scripture

because "the Holocaust challenged the notion that God could be both all-good and all-powerful. If God was all-good, then God could not be all-powerful because God did not intervene to stop the slaughter of innocent men, women, and children. If God was all-powerful, then God could not be all-good because God allowed or caused this evil to be perpetrated."[115]

Various conclusions were posited as the result of post-Holocaust reflections. Some suggested that God was dead. Others found a God who suffered with his people. Some believed that God was not all-good. Others took the position that God was not all-powerful—"I choose to think that God cannot stop us, however much God would like to do so."[116] Some interpreted the Holocaust as the voice of God. Others interpreted it as the silence of God. How does the Bible help interpret the origin of evil for you?

*Turn now to the next page
for Guided Exercise #8*

The State of Israel

Since the Jews had no homeland, they had no place to go during the Holocaust. The death of six million Jews created an obvious need for a secure place, which gave birth to the State of Israel. On May 14, 1948 the old dream of regaining the promised land was realized when Israel declared independence from Britain. This decision was met a few hours later by the invasion of Arab armies from Egypt, Syria, Jordan, Lebanon, Iraq, and Saudi Arabia.

A Natural History of Scripture

Guided Exercise #8

The classic question about the origin of evil is known as theodicy. This is not only an unsettling question, but also an unsettled question.

1. Genesis 1:1. "In the beginning God created the heavens and the earth." (Revised Standard Version). This traditional translation has been used by theologians to support the doctrine of creation out of nothing. If nothing was there, then God also created evil, which answers the question of the origin of evil.
2. Isaiah 45:7. "I form the light, and create darkness: I make peace, and create evil: I the LORD do all these things." (King James Version) For those who believe in an all-powerful God, here's a text for you. The paradox this leaves you with is answering whether or not God is all good, since he creates evil.
3. Genesis 1:1. "In the beginning when God created the heavens and the earth." This supports the doctrine of creation (order) out of chaos, which is honest with the text because it is modeled after the *Enuma Elish* . This lets evil be preexistent to creation and consequently lets God off the hook.
4. Job 28:28. "And he said to humankind, 'Truly, the fear of the Lord, that is wisdom; and to depart from evil is understanding." The book of Job is considered the classical exposition on the theodicy question. While it never tells the origin of evil, it recommends abstinence from it.

A Natural History of Scripture

Against impossible odds, the Jews prevailed. During the war, the United Nations arranged several cease-fires and the final one was declared in January 1949. In the end, Jerusalem was divided, with the Old City under Jordanian rule and the new City under Jewish control. This left the Western Wall, Judaism's holiest site, inaccessible until it was finally regained during the Six-Day War in 1967.

More Responses

The Revised Standard Version

By the 1800s scholars realized the King James Version had dated language and grave textual defects. In 1870 the English Revised Version was published with corrected mistranslations and thousands of changes based on new manuscript discoveries. In 1901 the American Standard Version was published with literal renderings of the Hebrew and Greek from the best possible ancient manuscripts.

The problem with the ERV and the ASV was that they were too mechanical and didn't flow. In 1937 a new revision was authorized to correct this problem. In 1946 the Revised Standard Version of the New Testament was published and in 1952 the RSV of the entire Bible was released. The RSV was met with much consternation by fundamentalists because it was honest with the text rather than catering to theological concerns. For example:

- Isaiah 7:14 now talked about a 'young woman' rather than a 'virgin.'

A Natural History of Scripture

- Colossians 1:14 no longer stated that redemption came 'through his blood.'
- John 7:53-8:11 now contained a footnote that the passage did not appear in most ancient manuscripts.
- Mark 16:9-20 became a footnote with the explanation that the oldest manuscripts ended with Mark 16:8.

Why all the fuss? Tradition is tough to beat. It would have been easier to leave the Bible alone, but the Revised Standard Version translators were committed to being honest with the text. They used the best Hebrew Bible and Greek New Testament available as the basis for their revision, whether it meant popular acceptance or not. When translation into English was difficult, they commonly offered a footnote of alternative possibilities.

TANAKH

The Jewish Publication Society started in 1955 to translate the Hebrew Bible into modern English. In 1962 *The Torah* was published, followed in 1978 with the publication of *The Prophets* (or *Nevi'im* in Hebrew). In 1982 *The Writings* (or *Kethuvim* in Hebrew) made its way to the market and in 1985 all three volumes were published together as the *Tanakh* (an acronym for *Torah-Nevi'im-Kethuvim*). When translation was especially difficult, the committee of translators offered footnotes to explain the situation.

A Natural History of Scripture

The Postmodern Era

Whatever the Postmodern Era means, the one thing we know is that it follows the Modern Era. I personally see it as a transitional stage in history, much the same as the Enlightenment provided the transition to Modernity. Just as the French Revolution in 1789 finally gave birth to Modernity, I believe the fall of the Berlin Wall in 1989 finally gave birth to Postmodernity. One of the major events of the Postmodern Era has been the globalization of Christianity. This has played no small part in the virtual explosion of new translations and versions of the Bible.

Standardizing the Christian Text

The earliest New Testament manuscripts were in codex form (like our book form as opposed to the scroll format used for Jewish literature), which was very possibly an invention of Christianity. As these codices (plural of codex) "were used and reused, they were copied and recopied, in the churches and (later) in scriptoria, leaving for us a legacy of more than 5,000 Greek (manuscripts),"[117] none of which are the original copies.

There are some 300,000 variant readings among these New Testament manuscripts. Inadvertent errors (like mistaken word divisions, when there were no spaces or punctuation) and conscious improvements (like changes in grammar, spelling, and style) have created this situation which makes translation as much an art as a science. One biblical scholar described the problem well when he said, "there are more

A Natural History of Scripture

differences among our manuscripts than there are words in the New Testament."[118]

New Testament manuscripts were written in large, unconnected letters (uncials) until the tenth century, on both papyrus and parchment. From the ninth century on, cursive letters (minuscules) were used, written on parchment and paper. Although manuscripts were written on papyrus, parchment, or paper in uncial or in minuscule handwriting, they are classified in three categories: papyri, uncials, and minuscules. There are currently ninety-four different papyri, more than 260 different uncials, and more than 2,800 miniscules. The remaining Greek manuscripts are called lectionaries, which contain passages from the scriptures rather than books from the Bible.

The papyri and early uncials assume the position of prominence among New Testament manuscripts. Two groups stand out in importance: "the forty-three oldest papyri, plus the four oldest uncials, all of which date prior to the early fourth century; and the great uncial manuscripts of the fourth century, primarily Codices Sinaiticus, Alexandrinus, and Vaticanus, but also Codex Bezae of the late fourth/early fifth century and Codex Washingtonianus of the early fifth."[119] The papyri and the very earliest uncials are highly fragmentary, while the fourth/fifth century codices contain all or most of the New Testament.

*See the next three pages
for a listing of the
New Testament manuscripts.*[120]

A Natural History of Scripture

The effort of textual critics has at long last given us a standardized Christian text. They used 'best guess' efforts to try to establish as close as possible what the original Greek New Testament might have said. Remember that this has been done without one original letter, word, verse, paragraph, chapter, or book in existence. In 1993 the United Bible Societies published the fourth revised edition of the *Greek New Testament*.

Although the book is written in Greek, it can still be useful to the serious Bible student. Where uncertainty about the original text remains, the following footnote formula was employed: "The letter A indicates that the text is certain. The letter B indicates that the text is almost certain. The letter C, however, indicates that the Committee had difficulty in deciding which variant to place in the text. The letter D, which occurs only rarely, indicates that the Committee had great difficulty in arriving at a decision."[121] This represents the on-going formation of the Christian scriptures, which will continue to be revised and updated as more ancient manuscripts are discovered, shedding new light on the best possible text.

Ancient Manuscript Names

Symbol	Manuscript
$p^1...p^{115}$	The papyrus manuscripts are numbered in the order they were published
א	Codex Sinaiticus
A	Codex Alexandrinus

A Natural History of Scripture

B	Codex Vaticanus
C	Codex Ephraemi Rescriptus
D^{ea}	Codex Bezae
D^p	Codex Claromontanus
E^e	Codex Basilensis
E^a	Codex Laudianus
F^e	Codex Boreelianus
G^e	Codex Seidelianus I
G^p	Codex Boernerianus
H^e	Codex Seidelianus II
L^{ap}	Codex Angelicus
L^e	Codex Regius
P^{apr}	Codex Porphyrianus
T	Codex Borgianus
W	Codex Washingtonianus
X	Codex Monacensis
Z	Codex Dublinensis
Δ	Codex Sangallensis
Θ	Codex Coridethianus
Ψ	Codex Athous Lavrensis
M	Majority of manuscripts
f^1	Minuscules family 1
f^{13}	Minuscules family 13
Arm	Armenian versions
Cop	Coptic versions
cop^{bo}	Coptic Bohairic
cop^{fay}	Coptic Fayyumic
cop^{sa}	Coptic Sahidic
Eth	Ethiopic versions
Geo	Georgian versions
Goth	Gothic versions

A Natural History of Scripture

It	Old Latin versions
it^a	Old Latin Vercellensis
it^d	Old Latin Cantabrigiensis
it^e	Old Latin Palatinus
it^{gig}	Old Latin Gigas
it^k	Old Latin Bobiensis
Syr	Syriac versions
syr^c	Syriac Curetonian
syr^h	Syriac Harklean
syr^p	Syriac Peshitta
syr^{pal}	Syriac Palestinian
syr^s	Syriac Sinaiticus
MSS^N	The person named N reported having seen the given manuscript

Figure 12

A Natural History of Scripture

Conclusion
Future of the Bible

The Talmud was never completed, never officially declared finished, without need for additional material. The Bible, by comparison, underwent various stages of compilation and redaction, but was eventually completed, and it was categorically stated that no additions could be introduced."[122]

The above statement is a limited view of canonization. The following chart reveals a variety of additions by different religious groups.[123]

Religion	Hebrew Scriptures	Christian Sequel
Samaritans	5	0
Jews	39	0
Protestants	39	27
Catholics	46	27
Greek Orthodox	50	27
Slavonic	51	27
Other Eastern Churches	52	27
Ethiopian I	46	35
Ethiopian II	54	27

Figure 13

A Natural History of Scripture

This shows that the Bible we have today is an open canon. As world-renowned physicist Fritjof Capra says, "open systems develop and evolve,"[124] and the Bible is no different. Bibliogenesis happened four thousand years ago with the first oral stories, has evolved to what we have today through editing and research, and will continue to develop as archaeologists and textual critics make new discoveries.

Perhaps some of the Hebrew Scriptures that have long ago disappeared will be found,[125] or Paul's letter to the Laodiceans might be unearthed. Maybe the "Q" gospel will be discovered, or even a gospel in the original Aramaic language will turn up. One thing we know for sure, the Bible will never be finalized. The ebb and flow of discovery will help establish an ever-closer possibility of what the Bible says, but too many discrepancies exist to ever pronounce a completed text.

So does the Bible have a future? Of course it does. It is the best selling book of all time for a reason: it speaks to our innate need to understand how we fit into the big picture. This masterpiece of literature tells the story of the relationship between God and God's people. It is an on-going story and that is why we fit so well into the dialogue. Another reason the Bible has a future is because it will never die. Following the traditional doctrine about Jesus, I see the Bible as fully human and fully divine.

Fully Human/Fully Divine

"And the Word became flesh and lived among us...full of grace and truth" (John 1:14). Over the last four thousand years, the Word of God has indeed been born and has grown

A Natural History of Scripture

among us. The stories were nurtured in the womb of the Fertile Crescent, born and grew in the land of Palestine, and have continued to mature around the world. In this sense it is fully human, because it had a beginning. Many authors put the stories together, while others edited the stories, and still others eventually brought them to book form. There is nothing inherently holy about the book itself. It is simply words on paper. What makes it holy is its divine message.

The divine message of the Bible is that we will live forever, and the Bible itself participates in that promise: "The grass withers, the flower fades; but the word of our God will stand forever" (Isaiah 40:8). Although the Bible is fully human in many ways, it is also fully divine. Death cannot conquer it because it will live forever. As the invading Roman armies gave the Essene community a reality check that their end was near, the Essenes responded by protecting God's Word in clay jars in the caves of Quman by the Dead Sea.

This serves as a case study on the possibility of losing the Bible. When the famous Dead Sea Scrolls were discovered after nearly two thousand years of death and decay, it wasn't as if it needed resurrected to once again share its message. The Bible lived through those two thousand years without that little insurance package tucked away in Israel. Although the Bible became a very human book, which continues to dwell among us, its divinity is in its message. That message started in oral form some four thousand years ago, and will last as long as there is breath to share it.

A Natural History of Scripture

Bibliography

Aaland, Barbara, et. al., editors. *The Greek New Testament*, 4th revised edition. Stuttgart, Germany: United Bible Societies, 1994.

Akenson, Donald Harman. *Surpassing Wonder: The Invention of the Bible and the Talmuds*. New York: Harcourt, 1998.

_____. *Saint Saul: A Skeleton Key to the Historical Jesus*. New York: Oxford University Press, 2000.

Alexander, Patrick H., et. al., editors. *The SBL Handbook of Style: For Ancient Near Eastern, Biblical, and Early Christian Studies*. Peadbody, Massachusetts: Hendrickson, 1999.

Alter, Robert. *Canon and Creativity: modern writing and the authority of scripture*. New Haven: Yale University Press, 2000.

Anderson, Bernard W. *Understanding the Old Testament*. 2nd edition. Englewood Cliffs, New Jersey: Prentice-Hall, 1966.

Armstrong, Karen. *A History of God: The 4000-Year Quest of Judaism, Christianity and Islam*. New York: Knopf, 1994.

A Natural History of Scripture

_____. *In the Beginning: A New Interpretation of Genesis.* New York: Ballantine Books, 1996.

_____. *Jerusalem: One City, Three Faiths.* New York: Knopf, 1996.

Augustine. *City of God.* Translated by Gerald Walsh, et. al. New York: Doubleday, 1958.

Barash, David P. and Nanelle R. *Madame Bovary's Ovaries: A Darwinian Look at Literature.* New York: Delacorte Press, 2005.

Barton, John. "Redaction Criticism", *The Anchor Bible Dictionary*, vol. 5. New York: Doubleday, 1992.

Beck, Astrid Billes. "Introduction to the Leningrad Codex", *The Leningrad Codex: A Facsimile Edition.* Grand Rapids, Michigan: Eerdmans, 1998.

Biblia Hebraica. Stuttgart: German Bible Society, 1990.

Bloom, Harold. *The Western Canon: The Books and School of the Ages.* New York: Riverhead, 1994.

_____. *How to Read and Why.* New York: Scribner, 2000.

Boorstin, Daniel J. *The Discoverers: A History of Man's Search to Know His World and Himself.* New York: Vintage Books, 1983.

A Natural History of Scripture

_____. *The Seekers: The Story of Man's Continuing Quest to Understand His World.* New York: Random House, 1998.

Borg, Marcus, consulting editor. *The Lost Gospel Q: The Original sayings of Jesus.* Berkeley, California: Ulysees Press, 1996.

Braudel, Fernand. *Memory and the Mediterranean.* Translated by Sian Reynolds. New York: Knopf, 2001.

Brown, Raymond E. *An Introduction to the New Testament.* New York: Doubleday, 1997.

Cahill, Thomas. *Desire of the Everlasting Hills: The World before and after Jesus.* New York: Doubleday, 1999.

Carroll, James. *Constantine's Sword: The Church and the Jews: A History.* New York: Houghton Mifflin, 2001.

Carroll, Sean B. *Endless Forms Most Beautiful: The New Science of Evo Devo and the Making of the Animal Kingdom.* New York: W. W. Norton, 2005.

_____. *The Making of the Fittest: DNA and the Ultimate Record of Evolution.* New York: W. W. Norton, 2006.

Charlesworth, James H., editor. *The Old Testament Pseudepigrapha.* 2 vols. New York: Doubleday, 1983 and 1985.

A Natural History of Scripture

Chidester, David. *Christianity: A Global History.* San Francisco: Harper, 2000.

Cohen, Shaye J. D. *From the Maccabees to the Mishnah.* Philadelphia: Westminster Press, 1987.

Cohn-Sherbock, Lavinia and Dan. *A Short History of Judaism.* Rockport, MA: Oneworld, 1994.

Comfort, Philip W. *Essential Guide to Bible Versions.* Wheaton, Illinois: Tyndale, 2000.

Coogan, Michael D., editor. *The Oxford History of the Biblical World.* New York: Oxford University Press, 1998.

Crossan, John Dominic. *The Birth of Chrisitianity: Discovering What Happened in the Years Immediately After the Execution of Jesus.* San Francisco: Harper, 1998.

Diamond, Jared. *Guns, Germs, and Steel: The Fates of Human Societies.* New York: W. W. Norton & Company, 1998.

Durant. Will. *Heroes of History: A Brief History of Civilization from Ancient Times to the Dawn of the Modern Age.* New York: Simon & Schuster, 2001.

Ehrman, Bart D. *Jesus: apocalyptic prophet of the new millennium.* New York: Oxford University Press, 1999.

A Natural History of Scripture

_____. *The New Testament: A Historical Introduction to the Early Christian Writings*, 2nd ed. New York: Oxford University Press, 2000.

Epp, Eldon Jay. "Ancient Texts and Versions of the New Testament", *The New Interpreter's Bible*, vol. 8. Nashville: Abingdon, 1995.

Finkelstein, Israel, and Neil Asher Silberman. *The Bible Unearthed: Archaeology's New Vision of Ancient Israel and the Origin of Its Sacred Texts*. New York: The Free Press, 2001.

Fitzmyer, Joseph A. *The Semitic Background of the New Testament*. Combined edition. Grand Rapids, Michigan: Eerdmans, 1997.

Flanders, Henry Jackson, Jr., Robert Wilson Crapps, and David Anthony Smith. *People of the Covenant: An Introduction to the Hebrew Bible*, fourth edition. New York: Oxford University Press, 1996.

Fredricksen, Paula. *Jesus of Nazareth, King of the Jews: A Jewish Life and the Emergence of Christianity*. New York: Vintage, 1999.

Freedman, David Noel, editor. *The Anchor Bible Dictionary*. 6 vols. New York: Doubleday, 1992.

A Natural History of Scripture

_____. *The Nine Commandments: Uncovering a Hidden Pattern of Crime and Punishment in the Hebrew Bible.* New York: Doubleday, 2000.

Friedman, Richard Elliot. *Who Wrote the Bible?* San Francisco: Harper, 1987.

Gould, Stephen Jay. *The Structure of Evolutionary Theory.* Cambridge: The Belknap Press of Harvard University Press, 2002.

Grant, Michael. *The History of Ancient Israel.* London: Phoenix, 1984.

Greek New Testament, The. 4th edition. Stuttgart: German Bible Society, 1994.

Harrington. Daniel J. "Introduction to the Canon," *The New Interpreter's Bible*, vol. 1. Nashville: Abingdon, 1994.

Heidel, Alexander. *The Gilgamesh Epic and Old Testament Parallels.* 2nd edition. Chicago: The University of Chicago Press, 1949.

_____. *The Babylonian Genesis.* 2nd edition. Chicago: The University of Chicago Press, 1951.

Heschel, Abraham J. *God in Search of Man: A Philosophy of Judaism.* New York: Farrar, Straus & Giroux, 1976.

A Natural History of Scripture

Jagersma, Henk. *A History of Israel from Alexander the Great to Bar Kochba*. Philadelphia: Fortress Press, 1985.

Kirsch, Jonathan. *Moses: A Life*. New York: Ballantine, 1998.

Kugel, James L. *The Bible As It Was*. Cambridge, Mass.: Harvard University Press, 1997.

_____. *Great Poems of the Bible*: A Reader's Companion with New Translations. New York: The Free Press, 1999.

Latourette, Kenneth Scott. *A History of Christianity: Volume I: to A.D. 1500*, revised edition. Peadbody, MA: Prince Press, 1997.

Lebedev. Victor V. "The Oldest Complete Codex of the Hebrew Bible", *The Leningrad Codex: A Facsimile Edition*. Grand Rapids, Michigan: Eerdmans, 1998.

Leningrad Codex, The. A Facsimile Edition. Grand Rapids, Michigan: Eerdmans, 1998.

Maier, Paul L. *Josephus: The Essential Writings*. Grand Rapids, Michigan: Kregel, 1988.

_____. *Eusebius: the Church History*. Grand Rapids, Michigan: Kregel, 1999.

Man, John. *Gutenberg: How One Man Remade the World with Words*. New York: John Wiley & Sons, 2002.

A Natural History of Scripture

McGrath. Alister E. *In the Beginning: the Story of the King James Bible and How It Changed a Nation, a language, and a Culture.* New York: Doubleday, 2001.

Metzger, Bruce M., and Roland E Murphy, editors. *The New Oxford Annotated Bible with the Apocryphal/Deuterocanonical Books*, New Revised Standard Version. New York: Oxford University Press, 1991.

New Interpreter's Bible, The. 12 vols. Nashville, TN: Abingdon Press, 1994-2002.

Noll, Mark A. *Turning Points: Decisive Moments in the History of Christianity*, 2nd edition. Grand Rapids, Michigan: Baker Academic, 2000.

Nuesner, Jacob. *The Mishnah: A New Translation*. New Haven: Yale University Press, 1988.

Ouaknin, Marc-Alain. *Mysteries of the Alphabet: The Origins of Writing*. Translated by Josephine Bacon. New York: Abbeville Press, 1999.

Parrinder, Geoffrey, editor. *World Religions: From Ancient History to the Present*. New York: Facts on File, 1971.

Pelikan, Jaroslav. *The Vindication of Tradition*. New Haven: Yale University Press, 1984.

A Natural History of Scripture

Pelikan, Jaroslav, editor. *Sacred Writings, volume 3. Islam: The Qur'an.* Translated by Ahmed Ali. New York: Quality Paperback Book Club, 1992.

Pury, Albert de. "Yahwist ('J') Source", *The Anchor Bible Dictionary*, vol. 6. New York: Doubleday, 1992.

Roberts, J. M. *A Short History of the World.* New York: Oxford, 1997.

Robinson, James M., editor. *The Nag Hammadi Library.* Revised edition. San Francisco: Harper, 1990.

Rosenberg, David. *The Book of David: A New Story of the Spiritual Warrior and Leader Who Shaped Our Inner Consciousness.* New York: Three Rivers Press, 1997.

Sanders, James A. "Canon", *The Anchor Bible Dictionary*, vol. 1. New York: Doubleday, 1992.

Sarna, Nahum. *Understanding Genesis.* New York: Schocken, 1966.

Segal, Alan F. *Paul the Convert: The Apostolate and Apostasy of Saul the Pharisee.* New Haven: Yale University Press, 1990.

Seife, Charles. *Zero: The Biography of a Dangerous Idea.* New York: Viking, 2000.

Septuaginta. Stuttgart: German Bible Society. 1979.

A Natural History of Scripture

Shelley, Bruce L. *Church History in Plain Language*, 2nd ed. Nashville: Thomas Nelson, 1995.

Silberman, Neil Asher. *Heavenly Powers: Unraveling the Secret History of the Kabbalah*. Edison, NJ: Castle Books, 2000.

Talmud, The: Selected Writings. Translated by Ben Zion Bokser. New York: Paulist Press, 1989.

TANAKH: The Holy Scriptures. New York: The Jewish Publication Society, 1985.

Telushkin, Joseph. *Jewish Literacy: The Most Important Things to Know About the Jewish Religion, Its People, and Its History*. New York: Morrow, 1991.

_____. *Biblical Literacy: The Most Important People, Event, and Ideas of the Hebrew Bible*. New York: Morrow, 1997.

Trobisch, David. *The First Edition of the New Testament*. New York: Oxford University Press, 2000.

Vermes, Geza. *The Complete Dead Sea Scrolls in English*. New York: Penguin, 1997.

_____. *The Changing Faces of Jesus*. New York: Penguin Compass, 2002.

Vulgata, Biblia Sacra. Stuttgart: German Bible Society, 1994.

A Natural History of Scripture

Westermann, Claus. *Genesis 1-11*. Translated by John J. Scullion. Minneapolis: Fortress Press, 1994.

Williamson. Clark M. *Has God Rejected His People?* Nashville: Abingdon, 1982.

A Natural History of Scripture

Appendix A[1]
Context of the Hebrew Scriptures

BOOK	AUTHORS/ EDITORS	DATE	WRITTEN FROM
Genesis	J[2]	950 BC—922 BC	Jerusalem
	E[3]	850 BC—800 BC	Northern Kingdom
	P[4]	500 BC	Babylon
	R[5]	480 BC	Babylon
Exodus	J	950 BC—922 BC	Jerusalem
	E	850 BC—800 BC	Northern Kingdom
	P	500 BC	Babylon
	R	480 BC	Babylon
Leviticus	P	500 BC	Babylon
	R	480 BC	Babylon

[1] the following appendices contain some guesswork by the author concerning the "date" and "written from" categories.
[2] the (J)ahwistic tradition
[3] the (E)lohistic revision
[4] the (P)riestly source
[5] the Editor, or (R)edactor

A Natural History of Scripture

Numbers	J	950 BC—922 BC	Jerusalem
	E	850 BC—800 BC	Northern Kingdom
	P	500 BC	Babylon
	R	480 BC	Babylon
Deuteronomy	D[6]	700 BC—650 BC	Southern Kingdom
	R	480 BC	Babylon
Joshua	DH[7]	650 BC—600 BC	Southern Kingdom
	R	480 BC	Babylon
Judges	DH	650 BC—600 BC	Southern Kingdom
	R	480 BC	Babylon
1 Samuel	DH	650 BC—600 BC	Southern Kingdom
	R	480 BC	Babylon
2 Samuel	DH	650 BC—600 BC	Southern Kingdom
	R	480 BC	Babylon
1 Kings	DH	650 BC—600 BC	Southern Kingdom
	R	480 BC	Babylon
2 Kings	DH R	650 BC—600 BC 480 BC	Southern Kingdom Babylon
Isaiah 1-39	Isaiah	742 BC	Jerusalem

---

[6] the (D)euteronomic source
[7] the (D)euteronomistic (H)istorian

A Natural History of Scripture

Isaiah 40-55	Anonymous	540 BC	Babylon
56-66	Anonymous	400 BC	Jerusalem
	R	200 BC	Jerusalem
Jeremiah	Jeremiah	626 BC	Jerusalem
	R	200 BC	Jerusalem
Ezekiel 1-32	Ezekiel	590 BC	Jerusalem
33-48	Ezekiel	585 BC	Babylon
	R	200 BC	Jerusalem
Hosea	Hosea	745 BC	Northern Kingdom
	R	200 BC	Jerusalem
Joel	Joel	5th cent. BC	Jerusalem
	R	200 BC	Jerusalem
Amos	Amos	750 BC	Northern Kingdom
	R	200 BC	Jerusalem
Obadiah	Obadiah	5th cent. BC	Jerusalem
	R	200 BC	Jerusalem
Jonah	Jonah	5th cent. BC	Jerusalem
	R	200 BC	Jerusalem
Micah	Micah	730 BC	Moresheth
	R	200 BC	Jerusalem
Nahum	Nahum	612 BC	Southern Kingdom
	R	200 BC	Jerusalem
Habakkuk	Habakkuk	615 BC	Southern Kingdom
	R	200 BC	Jerusalem
Zephaniah	Zephaniah	636 BC	Southern Kingdom
	R	200 BC	Jerusalem

A Natural History of Scripture

Haggai	Haggai R	6th cent. BC 200 BC	Jerusalem Jerusalem
Zechariah 1-8 9-14	Zechariah Disciples R	6th cent. BC 4th cent. BC 200 BC	Jerusalem Jerusalem Jerusalem
Malachi	Malachi R	6th cent. BC 200 BC	Jerusalem Jerusalem
Psalms	Various R	1000 BC— 400 BC AD 90	Various Jamnia
Proverbs	Various R	961 BC— 300 BC AD 90	Various Jamnia
Job	Anonymous R	500 BC AD 90	Jerusalem Jamnia
Song of Solomon	Various R	3rd cent. BC AD 90	Jerusalem Jamnia
Ruth	Anonymous R	2nd cent. BC AD 90	Jerusalem Jamnia
Lamentations	Anonymous R	6th cent. BC AD 90	Babylon Jamnia
Ecclesiastes	Anonymous R	3rd cent. BC AD 90	Jerusalem Jamnia
Esther	Anonymous R	4th cent. BC AD 90	Jerusalem Jamnia
Daniel	Anonymous R	165 BC AD 90	Jerusalem Jamnia
Ezra	Ezra R	425 BC AD 90	Jerusalem Jamnia
Nehemiah	Nehemiah R	415 BC AD 90	Jerusalem Jamnia

A Natural History of Scripture

1 Chronicles	CH[8] R	400 BC AD 90	Jerusalem Jamnia
2 Chronicles	CH R	400 BC AD 90	Jerusalem Jamnia

---

[8] the (C)hronicler's (H)istory

A Natural History of Scripture

Appendix B
Context of the Christian Sequel

BOOK	AUTHORS/ EDITORS	DATE	WRITTEN FROM
Matthew	Disciple of Peter R	AD 90	Antioch
Mark	Disciple of Peter R	AD 70	Rome
Luke	Disciple of Paul R	AD 90	Greece
John	Disciple of John R	AD 98	Ephesus
Acts	Disciple of Paul R	AD 90	Greece
Romans	Paul R	AD 58	Corinth
1 Corinthians	Paul R	AD 57	Ephesus
2 Corinthians	Paul R	AD 57	Macedonia
Galatians	Paul R	AD 55	Ephesus
Ephesians	Disciple of Paul R	AD 95	Ephesus
Philippians	Paul R	AD 56	Ephesus
Colossians	Disciple of Paul R	AD 85	Ephesus

A Natural History of Scripture

1 Thessalonians	Paul R	AD 50	Corinth
2 Thessalonians	Disciple of Paul R	AD 95	Unknown
1 Timothy	Disciple of Paul R	AD 100	Rome
2 Timothy	Disciple of Paul R	AD 100	Rome
Titus	Disciple of Paul R	AD 100	Rome
Philemon	Paul R	AD 55	Ephesus
Hebrews	Disciple of Peter R	AD 85	Rome
James	Disciple of Peter R	AD 85	Palestine
1 Peter	Disciple of Peter R	AD 75	Rome
2 Peter	Disciple of Peter R	AD 110	Rome
1 John	Disciple of John R	AD 100	Ephesus
2 John	Disciple of John R	AD 100	Ephesus
3 John	Disciple of John R	AD 100	Ephesus
Jude	Disciple of Peter R	AD 95	Palestine
Revelation	Disciple of John R	AD 95	Patmos

A Natural History of Scripture

Glossary

Abraham—see Hebrew patriarchs.

adaptation—modification by natural selection of an organism which makes it better able to follow its way of life.

adolescent stage— the third stage in the process of biological development through which a single-celled egg gives rise to a complex animal.

adult stage— the fourth stage in the process of biological development through which a single-celled egg gives rise to a complex animal.

Amarna letters—cuneiform documents found in 1887 at Tell el-Amarna in Egypt, describing pre-Hebrew Canaan.

amoraim—traditional title for the rabbis living from about A.D. 200-500, who interpreted the Mishnah.

Ancient Near East—the land occupied today by Turkey, Syria, Lebanon, Israel, Jordan, Egypt, Saudi Arabia, Iraq, and Iran.

Apocrypha—scriptures with canonical status for Catholics, but not Jews or Protestants.

Aramaic—the primary international language from about 600 B.C.-A.D. 700.

A Natural History of Scripture

ark of the covenant—transportation vehicle for the two stone tablets of the Ten Commandments, as it made its way from Mt. Sinai to Jerusalem.

bibliogenesis—the beginning of the Bible.

biological development—the process through which a single-celled egg gives rise to a complex animal.

Canaan—land divinely promised to the Hebrew people.

canon—list of books deemed authoritative by different groups.

Christ—English word for the Greek translation of the Hebrew word Messiah.

Christian—term given by the Romans to designate those who believed Jesus was the Messiah, literally means "Christ follower."

Christian Sequel—Gospels, Letters, and Writings canonized by people of the Christian faith.

Chronicler's History—the author of 1 and 2 Chronicles, Ezra, and Nehemiah.

codex—major shift from scrolls to book form, possibly invented by the Christian movement.

common descent—see theory of common descent.

A Natural History of Scripture

Court Narrative—second Hebrew text, written during the divided monarchy in Judah, covering the life of King David.

Crusades—Christian attempt to free the Holy Land from Islam.

Dead Sea Scrolls—documents found in caves near the Dead Sea community of Qumran.

Deuteronomic source—fourth Hebrew text, written during the divided monarchy in Judah, covering a reinterpretation of the laws given during the exodus and calling for a centralization of worship in Jerusalem.

Deuteronomistic History—fifth Hebrew text, incorporating the full Court Narrative, telling the story from promised land to exile.

diversity—the range of variation in a group of related species.

Documentary Hypothesis—theory popularized by Julius Wellhausen, that views the Law as the editing of four literary documents, also known as the JEDP source theory.

Elohist source—third Hebrew text, written during the divided monarchy in Israel, covering the early history of the nation from the perspective of the northern kingdom.

Enuma Elish—Babylonian creation myth.

A Natural History of Scripture

epistle—letter addressed to a community.

Essenes—ascetic faction within Judaism, associated with the writing of the Dead Sea Scrolls.

evo-devo—the study of the evolution (as learned from paleontology) of development (as learned from biology).

evolution—see theory of evolution.

evolutionary developmental biology—"evo-devo" for short.

exile—time spent in Babylon by the Hebrew people after being conquered and deported.

exodus—Moses-led departure of the Hebrew people from captivity in Egypt. Literally means "path out."

Fertile Crescent—moon-shaped land extending from the Nile Valley to the Persian Gulf.

First Temple period—time between the building of Solomon's temple and It's destruction just prior to the exile.

Former Prophets—section of the Hebrew Scriptures containing the books of Joshua, Judges, Samuel, and Kings.

Gemara—rabbinic interpretation of the Misnah. Together they form the Talmud.

A Natural History of Scripture

Gentile—non-Jewish person.

Gilgamesh—Babylonian story that tells of a great flood.

gradualism—evolution by a slow accumulation of helpful mutations.

Hebrews—term describing the ancestors before Moses and Sinai.

Hebrew patriarchs—Abraham, Isaac, Jacob, and Joseph.

Hebrew Scriptures—the Law, Prophets, and Writings canonized by people of the Jewish faith.

Hellenism—the spread of Greek language, culture, and thought after the conquests of Alexander the Great and his successors.

infant stage—the second stage in the process of biological development through which a single-celled egg gives rise to a complex animal.

inheritance—the third of three basic facts about natural selection which states the genes of the parent will be passed on to the offspring.

Isaac—see Hebrew patriarchs.

A Natural History of Scripture

Israel—name God conferred on Jacob, literally means "wrestles with God;" a term describing the confederation of tribes that emerged after Sinai, and eventually settled in the land of Palestine; name of the northern kingdom centered around Samaria; name of the current nation, after gaining independence in 1948.

Jacob—see Hebrew patriarchs.

Jamnia—town where Rabbi Yohanan ben Zakkai reestablished Jewish communal life after the destruction of the Second Temple.

Jews—term describing the Hebrew ancestors after the exile.

Joseph—see Hebrew patriarchs.

Judah—name of the southern kingdom centered around Jerusalem.

Latter Prophets—the major prophets and the minor prophets.

L ORD—unique English spelling (small capitals) that informs the reader the Hebrew word it translates is the Tetragrammaton.

Maccabean revolt—successful war against the Seleucids by the Hasmonean family to regain Jewish control of the Holy Land in 167 B.C.

A Natural History of Scripture

macroevolution—large-scale patterns of evolution above the species level.

Major Prophets—Isaiah, Jeremiah, and Ezekiel.

Masada—natural fortress near the Dead Sea where a final holdout of Jewish rebels chose suicide over Roman enslavement after the destruction of the second temple.

Masoretic Text—authoritative text of the Hebrew scriptures compiled from A.D. 500 to A.D. 1000, abbreviated as MT.

Megillot—literally means "five scrolls." These Hebrew writings were read during associated Jewish holidays: Song of Solomon, Ruth, Lamentations, Ecclesiastes, and Esther.

Mesopotamia—literally means "land between the rivers."

Messiah—literally means "annointed." Refers to kings sent by God to reign over humanity. Christians believe Jesus was the long-awaited Messiah.

messianic Judaism—pre-Christian term for Jews who believed Jesus was the Messiah.

microevolution—small genetic changes that take place within a single species.

minuscules—Greek script written in small cursive letters.

A Natural History of Scripture

Minor Prophets— Hosea, Joel, Amos, Obadiah, Jonah, Micah, Nahum, Habbakuk, Zephaniah, Haggai, Zechariah, and Malachi; also called the Book of the Twelve.

Mishnah—codification of oral law, compiled about 200 A.D.

Monotheism—belief in the one God.

Mosaic law—613 written laws, recorded in the first five books of the Hebrew Scriptures.

Muslim Sequel—the Qur'an.

mutation—externally or internally caused changes in the sequence of DNA that leads to adaptations that may or may not be helpful to an organism.

Nag Hammadi Library—collection of gnostic writings discovered in 1945 in the Nag Hammadi region of Egypt.

natural selection—process where some natural variants of a species are favored because they are better suited to a changing local environment. Since inheritance exists, the offspring of survivors will tend to resemble their successful parents. The accumulation of favorable variations through time produces evolutionary change.

nomina sacra—sacred names written in shorthand.

oral law—rabbinic interpretations of Mosaic law.

A Natural History of Scripture

overproduction of offspring—the first of three basic facts about natural selection that states all organisms produce more offspring than can survive. Darwin called this superfecundity.

Palestine—land bridge between the Syrian Desert and the Mediterranean Sea, linking the continents of Europe, Asia, and Africa.

papyri—writing material made from the pith of the papyrus plant.

Pauline—having to do with Paul.

Petrine—having to do with Peter.

Pharaoh—king of Egypt.

Pharisees—faction within Judaism that accepted the oral law as holy.

Philistines—originating from Crete, these were part of the Sea Peoples who invaded Syria, Palestine, and Egypt.

Polytheism—belief in many gods.

prenatal stage—the first stage in the process of biological development through which a single-celled egg gives rise to a complex animal.

A Natural History of Scripture

Priestly source—Hebrew document written after the exile. Major source of material in the book of Leviticius, and minor source of material in the books of Genesis, Exodus, and Numbers.

Primary History—the Law and the Former Prophets, which together tell the full story from creation to promised land to exile.

Pseudepigrapha—"false writings" excluded by both the Jews and the Christians.

Q gospel—(from German *Quelle*, which means source) Hypothetical lost document used by Matthew and Luke, but not by Mark.

Qur'an—muslim sequel to the Bible, sacred to the people of the Islamic faith.

rabbinic Judaism—the form of Judaism that survived the destruction of the temple.

Red (Reed) Sea—the preferable translation of *yam suf* is either "Reed Sea" or "Sea of Reeds."

Sadduccees—faction within Judaism that rejected the oral law.

Samaria—capital of the northern kingdom of Israel. After the fall of Samaria, the northern land of Israel became known as Samaria.

A Natural History of Scripture

Samaritans—after the northern land of Israel became known as Samaria, its inhabitants became known as Samaritans. These people wrote their own copy of the Penteteuch. In the time of Jesus, they were squeezed into an even smaller area between Galilee and Jerusalem.

Second Temple period—time between the rebuilding of the temple after the exile, and before its destruction by the Romans in A.D. 70.

Septuagint—Greek translation of the Hebrew Scriptures in 250 B.C. in Alexandria, abbreviated as LXX.

scroll—sheets of writing material sewn together and rolled into a cylindrical shape.

Solomon's temple—first temple built in Jerusalem by the son of King David.

Sumer—the southern part of Babylonia, as opposed to Akkad in the northern part of Babylonia.

Talmud—the Mishnah, with its interpretation, called the Gemara. The Mishnah can stand as a separate book; the Gemara can not. Also, there are two versions: the Babylonian Talmud (written in Babylon), and the Palestinian Talmud (written in Jerusalem).

A Natural History of Scripture

TANAKH—English version of the Hebrew Scriptures, it is an acronym for it's three sections: Torah (Law), Nevi'im (Prophets), and Kethuvim (Writings).

tannaim—scholars of the oral law.

Targum(im)—translation(s) of the Hebrew Scriptures into Aramaic.

Ten Commandments—divinely given words to Moses for the Hebrew people. Literally means "ten words."

tetragrammaton—the four Hebrew letters (YHWH) used to record God's name in Exodus 3:14.

theory of common descent—all life on earth evolved from a single origin.

theory of evolution—change caused by natural selection.

Torah—first five books of the Hebrew Scriptures, also called the Pentateuch.

uncials—Greek script written in block letters from the fourth to eighth centuries A.D.

united monarchy—Israel's time of kingship under Saul, David, and Solomon.

Ur—city in the eastern tip of the Fertile Crescent.

A Natural History of Scripture

variation—the second of three basic facts about natural selection which states that variation forged the great diversity of life from the beginning.

Vulgate—translation of the Bible into Latin.

Yahweh—scholarly guessed-at pronunciation of the divine name YHWH.

Yahwist source—first Hebrew text, written during the united monarchy in Jerusalem, covering the early history of the nation.

YHWH—the tetragrammaton, or "four letters" used to record God's name in Exodus 3:14.

Zohar—an important Jewish mystical work of the thirteenth century.

A Natural History of Scripture

Scriptural Index

Hebrew Scriptures
(Old Testament)

Genesis
1-11—27, 69, 222
1:1—xii, 68, 69, 202
1:1-2:3—xii, 68, 69
1:2—67
2:4-25—22, 66
2:7—23
2:8—23
2:9—23
2:18—24
2:21-22—24
6:5-8—25
6:19—68
7:1-5—25
7:7—25
7:10—25
7:12—25
7:16b—25
7:17-20—26
7:22-23—26
8:2b-3a—26
8:6—26
8:6-8—68
8:8-12—26
8:13b—27

8:20-22—27
12-50—27
12:1—5
12:1-4—4
12:1-8—18
12:4—6
12:7—6
12:10-20—32
15:3—82
16:4-14—32
20:1-18—32
21:1-3—6
21:8-21—32
21:22-34—32
22:1-4—33
25:20—6
25:26—6
26:26-33—32
28:10-19—6
28:10-22—33
31:47a—96
32:22-30—33
32:28—6
37—33
37:3—6
40-41—33
42-45—33
46-50—33
49—91

A Natural History of Scripture

Exodus
1:22—7
2:10—7
3:14—7, 138
5-13—33
5:1—7
12:41—82
14:5—8
14:19a—34
14:20a—34
14:25a—34
15:20-21—34
15:21—18
16:4—8
19:20—134
20:1-17—8
20:3—70
20:4—21, 70
20:7—71
20:8—71
20:12—71
20:16—71
20:17—71
21:12-14—18
24:1-2—34
24:3-8—34
24:9-11—34
25:8—8
32:1-33:11—34
32:8—70

Leviticus
24:10-17—71

Numbers
12:1-16—34
14:8a—27
15:32-36—71
21:14—278
22:2-24:25—34
24:17—149
27:18-19—8

Deuteronomy
4:44-28:68—35
21:18-21—71
22:22-29—18
29:1—35
31:14-15—34
31:23—34
34:1-12—34

Joshua
3:15-16—9
7:11—71
8:29—9
10:13—278
11—27
24—27

Judges
1:26—27

A Natural History of Scripture

2:11-12—10
5—18
20:4-5—71
21:25—11

1 Samuel
7:15—28
8:1—28
8:1-22—28
8:6—28
8:7—28
8:19—11
9:1-10:16—28
9:7—28
9:9—28
9:16—28
9:19—28
10:1—29
10:17-27—28
10:21—28
10:24—11
13:1—12
13:14—12
16:1-13—18
17:48-51—13
24:20—13
28:19—13
31:4—13

2 Samuel
2:4—13

2:8-9—13
5:3—14
9—30
11:2-4—71
11:27—14
21:19—13
24:1—78

1 Kings
1—30
2—27
2:24—15
3:9—15
5-7—16
8:18-19—16
11:4-5—15
11:41—278
12—27
12:4—29
12:24—30
12:30—29
14:19—278
14:24—30
14:25—27
14:29—278
15:12—41
17:1—39
19:16—39
21:1-14—71
22:46—41

A Natural History of Scripture

2 Kings
2:8—39
2:11—39
5:10—40
5:15—40
8:24—41
10:30—40
11:21—41
13:21—40
17:6—47
17:24—47
18:4—47
18:13—48
19:35—48
22:8—50
23:2-3—51
25:5-7—55
25:9—55

Isaiah
1-39—36, 43, 62
2:4—44
7:14—44, 46, 135, 203
9:6—44, 46
11:1—135
11:2—44, 46
11:9—52
14:4—46
14:12—46
24-27—271
34—271

38:5-8—45
39—62
40—62
40-48—60
40-55—60, 62, 86
40-66—60
40:1-2—60, 62
40:1-11—18
40:8—212
43:16-19—61
44:24-28—62
45:1—61
45:7—202
48:6-8—62
52:13-15—62
53:4-5—61
56-66—60, 271

Jeremiah
1:10—104
2:13—50
7:4—55
7:9—71
10:11—96
11:19—49
18:18—133
26:18—45
29:7—55
29:10—55
31:15—135
36:2—49

A Natural History of Scripture

37:11—54
52:29—55
52:31-34—59

Ezekiel
1-24—53
1-32—53
5:6-8—54
11:16—108
25-32—53
28:13—23
31:8-9—23
33-39—60
33-48—53, 60
37:14—60
40-48—60, 271
48:35—60

Hosea
1:2—43
9:17—43
11:1—135

Joel
2:13—75
2:28—76
3:10—76
3:20—76

Amos
5:21—42

5:24—42
7:10-17—42

Obadiah
1:10—74

Jonah
3:3—77
3:10—77
4:11—77

Micah
3:12—45
6:8—45

Nahum
1:2—52
3:19—53

Habakkuk
1:2—51
1:13—52
2:4—52, 118
2:14—52

Zephaniah
1:1—48
2:3—49

Haggai
1:4—64

A Natural History of Scripture

2:3—64
2:9—74
2:19—74

Zechariah
1-8—75
3:1-5—18
4:6—75
4:9—64
6:15—64
9-14—75, 271
9:9—75
9:13—75
13:7-9—75

Malachi
3:1—76
4:5—76

Psalms
1-41—271
42-72—271
73-89—271
90-106—271
90:4—148
107-150—271
121:1-2—24

Proverbs
23:13—84

Job
28:28—65, 202
38:1-15—18

Song of Solomon
1:1—85

Ruth
1:16—86
2:11-12—86
4:18-22—86

Lamentations
3:22—87
4:11—87

Ecclesiastes
1:1—87
1:14—88
2:24—88
7:1-12—18
8:2-4—87
12:9--87

Esther
9:28—89

Daniel
2:4b-7:28—96
3:1-30—98

A Natural History of Scripture

6:1-28—98
7:13-14—98
11:18—95
12:1-2—99

Ezra
1:2-3—63
1:8—63
3:2—63
4:3-4—63
4:8-6:18—96
5:16—63
6:8—64
7:12-26—96

Nehemiah
2:17—73
6:15—73
8:1—73, 133
12:27—73

1 Chronicles
21:1—78

2 Chronicles
33:10-13—78
36:23—78

Septuagint

Psalms
151—271

Isaiah
7:14—135

Pseudepigrapha

Jubilees
1:5—108

Dead Sea Scrolls

Temple Scroll
XLV:14—109

Apocrypha

1 Maccabbees
9:27—268

A Natural History of Scripture

Christian Sequel
(New Testament)

Matthew
1:18-23—135
2:13-15—135
2:16-18—135
2:19-23—135
3:7-10—119
4:12-16—134
5:1—134
5:17—134
6:9b-13—92
7:24—112
7:28—274
8:14-17—134
11:1—274
12:15-21—134
13:34-35—134
13:53—274
15:24—111
16:18—112
19:1—274
21:1-5—134
26:1—274
27:3-10—134

Mark
5:1—126
5:13—126
6:3—133
6:45—126
6:53—126
7:31—126
8:10—126
13—272
14:61-64—111
15:12-15—111
16:8—125, 204
16:9-20—204

Luke
1:1-2—136
3:7-9—119
5:5—136
23:34—136
23:43—136

John
1:14—211
2:13—274
2:23—274
6:4—274
6:35—139
7:2—139
7:53-8:11—139, 204
8:12—139
9:22—127
10:22—139
10:36—139
11:55—274
12:1—274

A Natural History of Scripture

13:1—274
18:4-8—139
18:28—274
18:39—274
19:14—274
20:31—139
21:1-25—139

Acts
1:1—136
2:22-24—140
9:1-19—113
9:2—272
11:26—111
12:12—124
16:9—114
18:1-4—117
19:9—272
19:23—272
20:1—118
20:2-5—118
22:4—272
24:14—272
24:22—272
28:31—136

Romans
1:4—140
1:17—118

1 Corinthians
5:9—117
7:1—117
10:14-22—117
11:17-34—117
13—117
15—272
15:5-7—113

2 Corinthians
2:1—118
2:4—118
7:5-7—118
13:1—118
13:2—118

Galatians
2:7-9—112
3:28—116
4:16—115

Ephesians
2:14—131

Philippians
2:5-8—116
2:9-11—117

Colossians
1:14—204

A Natural History of Scripture

1 Thessalonians
2:2—114
2:9—115
3:1—115
4—272

2 Thessalonians
2:1-2—131

1 Timothy
2:12—147

2 Timothy
3:16—147

Titus
1:5-9—146

Philemon
17—116

Hebrews
5:11—130
8:7—130

James
1:1—128
2:24—129

1 Peter
2:17—128

5:1—128
5:13—128

2 Peter
1:18—148
3:8—148
3:16—148

1 John
4:8—146
5:16—146

2 John
7—146
10—146

3 John
1—146
9-10—146

Jude
1—130
14-15—130

Revelation
1:9—137
1:11—137
7:9-17—137
13:3—137
13:8—137

A Natural History of Scripture

Muslim Sequel
(Qur'an)

2:87—165
2:97—164
3:3—165
4:157—165
4:171—168
4:172—168

9:5—165
10:34-37—168
17:15—165

JewishSequel
(Babylonian Talmud)

Qiddushin
49a—89

A Natural History of Scripture

General Index

1 Chronicles, see Chronicles
1 Corinthians, xvi, 117, 229, 250
1 John, xvii, 146, 154, 230, 253
1 Kings, see Kings
1 Peter, 128, 253
1 Samuel, see Samuel
1 Thessalonians, xvi, 114, 115, 229, 253
1 Timothy, xvii, 147, 230, 253
2 Chronicles, see Chronicles
2 Corinthians, xvi, 118, 229, 252
2 John, xvii, 146, 154, 230, 253
2 Kings, see Kings
2 Peter, 148, 154, 230, 253
2 Samuel, see Samuel
2 Thessalonians, xvii, 131, 230, 253
2 Timothy, xvii, 147, 148, 230, 253
3 John, xvii, 146, 154, 230, 253

Abraham, xiii, 5, 6, 22, 32, 57, 164, 168, 234,
Acts, xvii, 100, 136, 140, 154, 229, 252
Adam, 22,
adaptation, xxiii, 109
agents of selection, xxiii, 2, 144, 145
Alexander the Great, 57, 79, 234
Alexandria, xvi, 83, 89, 132, 160, 240
Amos, xiv, 36, 41, 42, 43, 104, 106, 225, 236, 247
Apocrypha, xii, xviii, 114, 146, 157, 158, 159, 179, 230
Arabs, xviii, 163, 167
Armageddon, xxi
Assyria, xiv, 42, 44, 47, 50, 52
Athanasius, xviii, 160
Baal, 39, 40
Babylon, xv, xvi, xxiii, 46, 47, 48, 54, 55, 57, 58, 59, 61, 63, 66, 67, 73, 79, 97, 98, 128, 167, 170, 224, 225, 226, 227, 234, 241

A Natural History of Scripture

Bar Kokhba, xvii, 149
Bible, ix, xi, xix, xx, xxi, xxii, xxiii, xxiv, 2, 3, 4, 5, 8, 9, 11, 12, 16, 21, 23, 28, 29, 35, 40, 41, 46, 72, 79, 80, 81, 82, 84, 85, 89, 91, 102, 118, 131, 132, 133, 138, 143, 147, 157, 158, 171, 176, 180, 182, 184, 185, 187, 188, 189, 191, 192, 195, 196, 199, 201, 203, 204, 205, 206, 207, 210, 211, 212, 232, 240, 243
Boaz, 86
Caesar, 109
Calvin, 186
canon, xxi, xxii, xxiii, 72, 75, 84, 105, 113, 132, 133, 143, 150, 157, 158, 160, 179, 187, 211, 232
Chaldeans, 54
Charlemagne, 169
Charles Darwin, xix, 194
Christian Sequel, xvii, xviii, xix, xx, 91, 105, 109, 110, 112, 147, 148, 152, 153, 154, 160, 186, 229
Christians, 45, 46, 90, 100, 124, 127, 132, 137, 153, 155, 157, 160, 166, 173, 175, 176, 181, 192, 195, 200, 232
Chronicler's History, xv, 78, 79, 232
Chronicles, 8, 78, 79, 90, 95, 227, 232, 250
closed canon, xix, 187
Colossians, xvii, 129, 130, 229, 252
Constantine, 156, 157
Constantinople, xviii, 157, 161, 162, 163, 169, 170, 172, 174, 178
Council of Trent, xix, 186, 187
Court Narrative, xiv, 30, 36, 233
Cuneiform, xiii, 231
Daniel, xvi, 90, 91, 97, 98, 227, 249
David, xiii, 9, 10, 12, 13, 14, 15, 22, 30, 36, 44, 55, 71, 78, 86, 87, 99, 149, 153, 233, 241, 242
Dead Sea Scrolls, xii, xvi, xix, 99, 100, 108, 113, 132, 212, 222, 233, 234, 250
Deuteronomic source, xiv, 35, 36, 70, 233

A Natural History of Scripture

Deuteronomistic History, xiv, 8, 35, 36, 58, 70, 78, 233
Deuteronomy, 35, 50, 58, 70, 73, 90, 197, 198, 225, 245
Didache, 154
di-mester, xxii, 5, 9, 16
Ecclesiastes, xvi, 87, 90, 92, 95, 132, 227, 237, 249
Egypt, xiii, xxi, xxiii, 5, 6, 7, 10, 19, 29, 33, 48, 54, 59, 79, 82, 83, 89, 94, 135, 150, 170, 174, 201, 231, 234, 238, 239
Elijah, xiv, 39, 76
Elisha, xiv, 39, 40
Elohist source, xiv, 32, 33, 34, 36, 70, 232
Enuma Elish, xii, 67, 68, 202, 233
Ephesians, xvii, 130, 131, 229, 252
Epic of Gilgamesh, see Gilgamesh
Erasmus, xix, 181, 183
Essenes, 98, 99, 100, 132, 133, 212, 234
Esther, xvi, 85, 88, 90, 95, 132, 227, 237, 249
Evo-Devo, xxi, 233
evolution, xi, xxi, xxii, xxiii, xxiv, 2, 5, 12, 20, 41, 58, 81, 109, 143, 179
evolutionary biology, xxi, xxii, xxiv
exodus, xiii, 5, 11, 16, 36, 60, 62, 70, 89, 139, 234, 234
Exodus, 5, 27, 65, 70, 71, 73, 224, 240, 245
Ezekiel, xiv, xv, 51, 53, 60, 104, 105, 107, 132, 226, 237, 248
Ezra, xv, 73, 78, 83, 86, 96, 133, 227, 232, 250
Former Prophets, xv, 70, 73, 103, 104, 234, 240
Galatians, xvi, 115, 229, 252
Genesis, xii, 5, 65, 68, 70, 73, 78, 90, 171, 214, 221, 223, 240, 244
Gilgamesh, xiii, 67, 68, 218, 235
Gnostics, xviii, 150
Gomer, 43
Gospel, xxiii, 109
gradualism, 58, 109, 146
Greeks, xv, 75, 79, 81, 89

A Natural History of Scripture

Habbakuk, xiv, 51, 104, 106, 225, 236
Haggai, xv, 64, 74, 104, 106, 226, 236, 247
Hebrew Scriptures, xvi, xvii, xviii, 8, 23, 51, 52, 57, 66, 68, 79, 89, 91, 96, 98, 104, 119, 127, 132, 133, 135, 137, 147, 148, 150, 153, 157, 160, 169, 170, 176, 181, 199, 210, 211, 234, 235, 238, 241, 242, 244
Hebrews, xiii, xvii, 2, 8, 57, 67, 70, 129, 130, 154, 187, 230, 235, 253
Hellenism, 57, 83, 235
Herod, xvi, 109
historians, xxii, 20, 119
Holocaust, xix, 200, 201
Hosea, xiv, 36, 41, 42, 43, 104, 106, 135, 226, 238, 248
Isaac, xiii, 5, 6, 33, 57, 168, 235
Isaiah, xiv, xv, 36, 43, 44, 48, 60, 61, 62, 86, 104, 105, 225, 226, 237, 247
Israel, xiv, xx, xxi, 4, 5, 6, 10, 11, 13, 14, 15, 22, 23, 27, 28, 30, 32, 33, 36, 39, 40, 41, 42, 43, 45, 46, 47, 49, 50, 53, 59, 60, 62, 63, 64, 70, 73, 76, 77, 78, 84, 86, 100, 124, 133, 135, 153, 162, 167, 169, 198, 201, 212, 218, 231, 236, 240, 241, 242
Israelite, xiii, 10, 29, 31, 33, 40, 42, 86
Jacob, xiii, 5, 6, 33, 57, 74, 236
James, xvi, xvii, 65, 111, 113, 128, 130, 154, 230, 253
Jeremiah, xiv, 49, 55, 71, 104, 105, 135, 226, 237, 247
Jerome, xviii, 46, 157, 160, 181, 196
Jerusalem, xv, xvi, xviii, xxi, 9, 11, 14, 15, 29, 36, 41, 43, 45, 48, 49, 53, 54, 55, 60, 61, 62, 63, 66, 73, 74, 75, 76, 86, 87, 97, 101, 102, 105, 111, 112, 118, 123, 148, 149, 152, 164, 167, 168, 171, 173, 174, 203, 214, 224, 225, 226, 227,

Page 258

A Natural History of Scripture

228, 232, 233, 236, 241, 243
Jesus, xii, xvi, xxiii, 46, 59, 109, 110, 111, 112, 113, 116, 117, 119, 124, 125, 126, 127, 128, 129, 130, 131, 132, 133, 134, 135, 136, 138, 139, 140, 141, 142, 148, 150, 153, 157, 160, 163, 165, 168, 175, 176, 186, 211, 213, 215, 216, 217, 222, 232, 237, 241
Jewish Sequel, 254
Jezebel, 39, 40, 71
Job, xv, 65, 90, 227, 249
Joel, xv, 75, 104, 106, 226, 238, 248
John, xvi, xvii, 111, 124, 137, 138, 139, 140, 146, 154, 155, 229, 251
Jonah, xv, 76, 77, 86, 104, 106, 226, 238, 248
Joseph, xiii, 6, 7, 33, 57, 236
Josephus, xvii, 123, 219
Joshua, xiii, 8, 9, 10, 11, 27, 34, 36, 57, 70, 73, 225, 234, 245
Judah, xiv, 13, 29, 30, 32, 36, 41, 42, 43, 47, 48, 49, 53, 54, 55, 57, 59, 61, 62, 63, 76, 98, 198, 233, 236
Judahites, 30, 35, 51, 55, 57, 59, 111
Jude, xvii, 130, 154, 187, 230, 253
Judea, xvi, 104, 109, 110
Judges, xiii, 8, 10, 11, 36, 57, 70, 73, 89, 90, 225, 234, 245
Julius Wellhausen, xix, 197, 233
Justinian, 162, 163
Karl Marx, 194
King Ahab, 39
King Cyrus, 61, 63, 64
King Hezekiah, xiv, 44, 48
King James, 187, 188, 189
King Josiah, xiv, 48, 49, 50, 51
King Nebuchadnezzar, 54
Kings, 8, 31, 39, 41, 42, 43, 46, 57, 61, 62, 70, 73, 78, 90, 127, 174, 225, 234, 246, 247
Lamentations, xvi, 85, 86, 95, 227, 237, 249

Latin, xviii, 46, 96, 157, 162, 172, 174, 176, 181, 184, 185, 187, 196, 243
Law, xv, xxiii, 18, 51, 70, 72, 73, 84, 103, 108, 109, 130, 132, 133, 134, 139, 153, 160, 166, 233, 235, 239, 240, 242
Leviticus, 65, 70, 73, 90, 198, 224, 245
LORD, 6, 7, 8, 9, 10, 11, 12, 14, 15, 22, 23, 24, 25, 27, 30, 34, 35, 39, 40, 43, 44, 45, 48, 49, 50, 51, 52, 53, 55, 60, 61, 63, 64, 73, 75, 76, 77, 78, 86, 87, 133, 189, 202
Luke, xvii, 119, 120, 136, 140, 150, 229, 240, 251
Maccabean revolt, xvi, 83, 88, 97, 236
macroevolution, xxiii, 143
Maimonides, 174, 175, 181
Major Prophets, 104, 105, 237
Malachi, xv, 76, 104, 106, 158, 227, 238, 249
Marcion, xviii, 149
Mark, xvii, 119, 124, 125, 126, 134, 138, 140, 229, 240, 251
Martin Luther, xix, 158, 182, 183, 187
Masada, xvii, 107, 237
Masoretes, xviii, 171
Mattathias, 97
Matthew, xvii, 112, 119, 120, 129, 133, 134, 135, 140, 229, 240, 251
Mendelssohn, 191
Mesopotamia, xxi, 5, 94, 104, 149, 237
Micah, xiv, 36, 43, 45, 48, 104, 106, 226, 238, 248
microevolution, xxiii, 143
Minor Prophets, 104, 106, 238
minuscules, 206, 237
Mishnah, xviii, 153, 166, 167, 169, 216, 220, 231, 238, 241
monarchy, xiii, 11, 12, 14, 16, 29, 36, 38, 64, 78, 99, 193, 233, 242, 243
monotheism, 1, 22, 23, 40, 61, 69, 112
Moses, xiii, 7, 8, 9, 10, 11, 21, 33, 34, 35, 47, 57, 73, 85, 99, 103, 108,

A Natural History of Scripture

133, 134, 165, 196, 197, 198, 218, 234, 235, 242
Mount Sinai, 8, 21, 35, 85, 134
Muhammad, xviii, 163, 164, 165, 167, 168, 183
Muslim Sequel, xviii, 145, 238, 240, 254
Muslims, xviii, 32, 173, 178
Naaman, 40
Nag Hammadi, xii, xix, 150, 151, 221, 238
Nahum, xiv, 51, 52, 53, 104, 106, 226, 238, 248
Nehemiah, xv, 73, 78, 86, 227, 232, 250
Nineveh, 52, 53, 68, 77
northern kingdom, 29, 32, 34, 36, 41, 47, 63, 198, 233, 236, 240
Numbers, 5, 27, 65, 70, 73, 225, 240, 245
Obadiah, xv, 74, 104, 106, 226, 238, 248
oral tradition, 39, 98, 153
Palestine, xv, xxi, xxiii, 73, 79, 83, 94, 95, 104, 105, 107, 110, 130, 137, 148, 166, 170, 174, 189, 199, 212, 230, 236, 239

Papyrus, xiii
Patmos, xvii, 137, 230
Paul, xvi, xvii, 50, 111, 112, 113, 114, 115, 116, 117, 118, 124, 129, 130, 131, 133, 136, 140, 146, 147, 148, 149, 150, 154, 160, 211, 221, 229, 230, 239
Persia, xv, 61, 63, 64, 79
Peter, xvi, xvii, 111, 112, 113, 124, 128, 138, 148, 154, 163, 173, 229, 230, 239, 253
Pharisees, 98, 99, 239
Philemon, xvi, 115, 229, 252
Philippians, xvi, 116, 229, 252
Pontius Pilate, xvi, 110
Priestly source, xv, 58, 240
prophecy, xxii, 38, 45, 46, 53, 76, 84, 85, 107, 134, 135, 161
prophets, xxii, 10, 11, 20, 36, 37, 38, 39, 40, 41, 43, 48, 59, 64, 65, 70, 75, 76, 103, 134, 137, 158, 236
Proverbs, xv, 84, 92, 95, 132, 227, 249

A Natural History of Scripture

Psalms, 77, 94, 95, 227, 249
Pseudepigrapha, xii, xvi, 90, 91, 92, 93, 114, 215, 240, 250
Pythagoras, 67
Qumran, xvii, xix, 95, 99, 100, 132, 233
Rashi, 172
Rehoboam, 29, 30, 31, 41
Revelation, xvii, 46, 91, 137, 154, 187, 230, 253
Revised Standard Version, xx, 203, 204
Romans, xvi, xxiii, 81, 83, 95, 104, 105, 109, 110, 118, 123, 127, 130, 137, 149, 192, 229, 232, 241, 252
Rome, xvi, xviii, 95, 104, 117, 124, 128, 129, 136, 137, 146, 147, 148, 150, 155, 156, 161, 162, 163, 169, 172, 173, 229, 230
Ruth, xvi, 85, 86, 89, 95, 227, 237, 249
Sadduccees, 98, 99, 240
Samaria, 47, 236, 241
Samson, 10
Samuel, 8, 11, 12, 13, 28, 36, 70, 73, 78, 89, 225, 234, 246
Saul, xiii, 11, 12, 13, 28, 113, 213, 221, 242
Seleucid, 95, 99, 104
Septuagint, xii, xvi, xviii, xxiii, 89, 90, 94, 118, 132, 135, 157, 160, 170, 241, 250
Sheshbazzar, xv, 63
Solomon, xiii, 12, 14, 15, 16, 29, 74, 78, 85, 87, 234, 241, 242
Song of Solomon, xvi, 85, 95, 227, 237, 249
St. Augustine, 161
Sumerians, 19
Talmuddim, xviii, 145, 166
Tanakh, xx, 204
Targumim, xvi, xxiii, 94
temple, xiii, xv, xvii, 15, 16, 29, 41, 45, 51, 55, 60, 63, 64, 66, 74, 75, 76, 77, 78, 85, 95, 97, 105, 107, 108, 109, 111, 123, 127, 128, 131, 139, 153, 234, 236, 240, 241
textus receptus, 196, 200
the "Q" gospel, xvi, 119, 120

A Natural History of Scripture

the adolescent stage, xxii, 56
the adult stage, xxiii, 143
the Assyrian Empire, 47, 48
the Christian Sequel, see Christian Sequel
the Crusades, xviii, 173
the Dispersion, 57
the Documentary Hypothesis, xix, 196, 197
the evolution of development, xxi
the Fertile Crescent, xxi, xxii, 16, 19, 212, 242
the Flood, 24
the French Revolution, xix, 192
the Great Schism, xviii, 172
the Hebrew Bible, xix, xx, 199
the Holocaust, xix, 200, 201
the Holy Land, 66, 108, 128, 173, 174, 193, 199, 233, 236
the infant stage, xxii, 19
the Jewish Sequel, see Jewish Sequel
the Leningrad Codex, 171, 199, 214
the Masoretic Text, xviii, 171
the Megillot, 84, 86, 89
the Muslim Sequel, see Muslim Sequel
the overproduction of offspring, 2
the prenatal stage, xxii, 1
the promised land, xv, xviii, 8, 10, 14, 36, 57, 60, 62, 201
the Protestant Reformation, xix, 158, 182, 186
the Qur'an, 164, 165, 167, 179, 183, 238
the Ten Commandments, 8, 15, 16, 21, 71, 232
the ten tribes, xiv, 29, 57, 59
the theory of common descent, 4
the united monarchy, 12
Thomas Aquinas, 175
Titus, xvii, 118, 146, 230, 253
uncials, 206, 242
Vulgate, xviii, 157, 184, 187, 196, 243

A Natural History of Scripture

Wesley, 192
William Tyndale, xix, 184
Yahwist source, xiv, 22, 23, 24, 27, 29, 30, 32, 33, 34, 36, 70, 220, 243
Zechariah, xv, 31, 64, 75, 104, 106, 227, 238, 249

Zephaniah, xiv, 48, 49, 104, 106, 226, 238, 248
Zerubbabel, xv, 63, 64, 74, 75, 77, 108
Zohar, 175, 243
Zwingli, 183, 184

A Natural History of Scripture

Endnotes

Introduction

[1] Abraham Joshua Heschel, *God in Search of Man: A Philosophy of Judaism* (New York: Farrar, Straus & Giroux), 242.

[2] Sean B. Carroll, *The Making of the Fittest: DNA and the Ultimate Forensic Record of Evolution* (New York: W. W. Norton), 193. See also his excellent introductory book *Endless Forms Most Beautiful: The New Science of Evo Devo and the Making of the Animal Kingdom*.

[3] Harold Bloom, *How to Read and Why*, (New York: Scribner), 29.

Part One--Prenatal Stage: Storytellers

[4] David P. and Nanelle R. Barash, *Madame Bovary's Ovaries: A Darwinian Look at Literature* (New York: Delacorte Press), 21.

[5] Jonathan Kirsch argues in his book *God Against the Gods: The History of the War Between Monotheism and Polytheism* (New York: Viking Compass), 25-26, that Akhenaton deserves the credit for inventing monotheism because the Egyptians worshipped the one god Aton. His argument doesn't hold

A Natural History of Scripture

because monotheism has always been about the worship of God. Akhenaton's unique rejection of all other gods might deserve him credit for the invention of monoidolism, but that is a far cry from monotheism.

Chapter 1--Oral History: The Theory of Common Descent

[6] Charles Darwin, *The Origin of Species: by Means of Natural Selection or the Preservation of Favoured Races in the Struggle for Life* (Edison, NJ: Castle Books), 669-70.

[7] All scripture references are from the New Revised Standard Version (NRSV) of the Bible, unless otherwise specified.

[8] I have chosen to use a masculine term for God, but it should be noted that God is spirit and not limited to gender identification.

[9] For capitalization and spelling of biblical terms, I used the guidelines from the Society of Biblical Literature: Patrick H. Alexander, et. al., editors, *The SBL Handbook of Style: For Ancient Near Eastern, Biblical, and Early Christian Studies* (Peabody, Massachussetts: Hendrickson), 153-64.

[10] Rabbi Joseph Telushkin, *Biblical Literacy: The Most Important People, Events, and Ideas of the Hebrew Bible* (New York: William Morrow), 125.

A Natural History of Scripture

[11] James L. Kugel, *The Great Poems of the Bible: A Reader's Companion with New Translations* (New York: The Free Press), 146.

[12] Henry Jackson Flanders, Robert Wilson Crapps, and David Anthony Smith, *People of the Covenant: An Introduction to the Hebrew Bible*, fourth edition (New York: Oxford University Press), 263.

[13] Israel Finkelstein and Neil Asher Silberman, *The Bible Unearthed: Archaeology's New Vision of Ancient Israel and the Origin of Its Sacred Texts* (New York: The Free Press), 128.

[14] Finkelstein and Silberman, 129.

[15] How your translation deals with this problem says a lot about the theology of the translators. The New Revised Standard Version offers an explanatory footnote. Check to see how your favorite Bible deals with it.

Part Two--Infant Stage: Storytellers

[16] Marc-Alain Ouaknin, *Mysteries of the Alpahbet: The Origins of Writing* (New York: Abbeville Press), 18.

[17] Jared Diamond, *Guns, Germs, and Steel: The Fates of Human Societies* (New York: W. W. Norton & Company), 25. He goes on to identify the advantages of this part of the Fertile

A Natural History of Scripture

Crescent: 1) the climate produced annual plants that were edible by humans, including six of the modern world's twelve major crops; 2) the wild ancestors of many Fertile Crescent crops were already abundant and highly productive, so few changes were needed to cultivate them; 3) it had a high percentage of self-pollinating plants, which was convenient for early farmers, 136-38.

Chapter 2--Written History: Earliest Fossils in the Bible

[18] Donald Harman Akenson, *Surpassing Wonder: The Invention of the Bible and the Talmuds* (New York: Harcourt Brace & Company), 526.

[19] *Yahweh* is a scholarly guessed-at spelling of the divine name YHWH, the so-called Tetragrammaton (meaning four letters). Jehovah is a commonly guessed-at spelling of the divine name, but it comes from a historical mistake. When Hebrew received vowels (about 1000 AD), the scribes inserted the vowels from *adonai (a-o-a)*, the Hebrew word for Lord, between the consonants, resulting in *YaHoWaH*. Not knowing this tradition, later scribes thought this was God's name and it was ultimately corrupted in English to Jehovah.

[20] Nahum M. Sarna, *Understanding Genesis: The World of the Bible in the Light of History* (New York: Schocken Books), 24.

[21] Sarna, 25.

A Natural History of Scripture

[22] Sarna, 27.

[23] Albert de Pury, "Yahwist ('J') Source", *The Anchor Bible Dictionary*, vol. 6 (New York: Doubleday), 1,016.

[24] Metzger and Murphy, *The New Oxford Annotated Bible with the Apocrypha/Deuterocanonical Books* (New York:Oxford University Press), 338-39 OT.

[25] David Rosenberg, *The Book of David: A New Story of the Spiritual Warrior and Leader Who Shaped Our Inner Consciousness* (New York: Three Rivers Press), 73-111.

[26] The traditional translation of *yam suf* as the Red Sea is rejected by most contemporary scholars, based on the fact that *suf* is the same word that shows up in Exodus 2:3-5. There the baby Moses was put in a little ark and placed among the "reeds." For this reason, the preferable translation of *yam suf* is either "Reed Sea" or "Sea of Reeds."

[27] Flanders, et. al., 90.

Chapter 3--Prophets: First Branch of a New Species

[28] Will Durant, *Heroes of History: A Brief History of Civilization from Ancient Times to the Dawn of the Modern Age* (New York: Simon & Schuster), 58.

A Natural History of Scripture

Part Three--Infant Stage:Editors

[29] Finkelstein and Silberman, 47.

Chapter 4--Priests: Gradualism in Action

[30] David Noel Freedman, *The Nine Commandments: Uncovering the Hidden Pattern of Crime and Punishment in the Hebrew Bible* (New York: Doubleday), 180.

[31] The slow demise of prophecy is mentioned in several different sources. One of them is the Apocrypha: "So there was great distress in Israel, such as had not been since the time that prophets ceased to appear among them" (1 Maccabees 9:27).

[32] Kugel, 81-2.

[33] Karen Armstrong, *A History of God: The 4000-Year Quest of Judaism, Christianity and Islam* (New York: Knopf), 65.

[34] Charles Seife, *Zero: The Biography of a Dangerous Idea* (New York: Viking), 27.

[35] An excellent account of this story is Alexander Heidel's *The Babylonian Genesis* (Chicago: The University of Chicago Press), the chart can be found on page 129.

[36] Also see Alexander Heidel's *The Gilgamesh Epic and Old Testament Parallels*.

[37] Freedman, see above.

[38] Harold Bloom, *The Western Canon: The Books and School of the Ages* (New York: Riverhead Books), 3.

[39] Robert Alter, *Canon and Creativity: modern writing and the authority of scripture* (New Haven: Yale University Press), 4.

[40] James A. Sanders, "Canon", *The Anchor Bible Dictionary*, vol. 1 (New York: Doubleday), 840.

[41] Telushkin, 309.

[42] The Septuagint also had Psalm 151, but it was excluded from the Hebrew Scriptures during the canonization process.

[43] Book I: Psalms 1-41; Book II: Psalms 42-72; Book III: Psalms 73-89; Book IV: Psalms 90-106; Book V: Psalms 107-150.

[44] Metzger and Murphy, 503 OT.

Chapter 5--Translators: Diverstiy in Action

A Natural History of Scripture

[45] James L. Kugel, *The Bible As It Was* (Cambridge, Massachusetts: The Belknap Press of Harvard University Press), 18-23.

[46] Michael Grant, *The History of Ancient Israel* (London: Phoenix), 200.

[47] Henk Jagersma, *A History of Israel from Alexander the Great to Bar Kochba* (Philadelphia: Fortress Press), 27.

[48] Grant, 261.

[49] James H. Charlesworth, ed., *The Old Testament Pseudepigrapha*, vol. 1 (New York: Doubleday), 3.

[50] Ezek 40-48; Isa 24-27, 34, 56-66; Zech 9-14; Mark 13; 1 Thess 4; 1 Cor 15.

[51] Charlesworth, vi-vii (vol. 1), vi-viii (vol. 2).

[52] Metzger and Murphy, 1126 OT.

[53] Joseph A. Fitzmyer, "Essays on the Semitic Background of the New Testament", *The Semitic Background of the New Testament* (Grand Rapids, Michigan: Eerdmans), 288.

[54] Acts 9:2;19:9,23;22:4;24:14,22.

[55] Fitzmyer, 282.

A Natural History of Scripture

[56] Geza Vermes, *The Complete Dead Sea Scrolls in English* (New York: Penguin), vii xii.

[57] Sanders, 844.

Chapter 6--Evangelists: Adaptation at Work

[58] Bart D. Ehrman, *Jesus: apocalyptic prophet of the new millennium* (New York: Oxford University Press), 93.

[59] Paula Fredricksen, *Jesus of Nazareth, King of the Jews: A Jewish Life and the Emergence of Christianity* (New York: Vintage), 8.

[60] Alan F. Segal, *Paul the Convert: The Apostolate and Apostasy of Saul the Pharisee* (New Haven: Yale University Press), 4.

[61] Donald Harman Akenson, *Saint Saul: A Skeleton Key to the Historical Jesus* (New York: Oxford University Press), 15.

[62] Raymond E. Brown, *An Introduction to the New Testament* (New York: Doubleday), 471.

[63] Brown, 538.

[64] Marcus Borg, ed., *The Lost Gospel Q: The Original Sayings of Jesus* (Berkeley, California: Ulysses Press), 122-23.

[65] Paul L. Maier, *Josephus: The Essential Writings* (Grand Rapids, Michigan: Kregel), 382.

[66] Shaye J. D. Cohen, *From the Maccabees to the Mishnah* (Philadelphia: Westminster Press), 186.

[67] Book I ends at 7:28; Book II ends at 11:1; Book III ends at 13:53; Book IV ends at 19:1; Book V ends at 26:1. Note the similarity of these ending verses.

[68] Thomas Cahill, *Desire of the Everlasting Hills: The World before and after Jesus* (New York: Doubleday), 92.

[69] Brown, 809-10.

[70] John 2:13, 23; 6:4; 11:55; 12:1; 13:1; 18:28, 39; 19:14.

[71] Vermes' book is an exploration of the four favorite themes of his scholarly career: 1) the Jesus of John, who was mystical and divine; 2) the Christ of Paul, who was the mysterious Savior; 3) the Jesus of Acts, who was a prophet and Christ; 4) the Jesus of the Synoptics, who was a healer and teacher.

Part Four--Adult Stage: Standardizers

[72] Sean B. Carroll, *Endless Forms Most Beautiful*, 46.

A Natural History of Scripture

Chapter 7--Politicians: Natural Selection in Process

[73] Cohen, 192.

[74] Donald Harman Akenson, *Suprassing Wonder: The Invention of the Bible and the Talmuds* (New York: Harcourt Brace), 219.

[75] James M. Robinson, General Editor, *The Nag Hammadi Library in English* (San Francisco: Harper), 1.

[76] Robinson, v-viii.

[77] David Trobisch, *The First Edition of the New Testament* (New York: Oxford), 11.

[78] Trobisch, 38.

[79] Paul L. Maier, *Eusebius: the Church History* (Grand Rapids, Michigan: Kregel), 115.

[80] James Carroll, *Constantine's Sword: The Church and the Jews: A History* (New York: Houghton Mifflin), 168.

[81] Metzger and Murphy, iii AP.

[82] J. M. Roberts, *A Short History of the World* (New York: Oxford), 151.

A Natural History of Scripture

[83] David Chidester, *Christianity: A Global History* (San Francisco: Harper), 162.

[84] Lavinia and Dan Cohn-Sherbok, *A Short History of Judaism* (Oxford: Oneworld), 49.

[85] Karen Armstrong, *Jerusalem: One City, Three Faiths* (New York: Knopf), 220.

[86] Joseph Telushkin, *Jewish Literacy: The Most Important Things to Know About the Jewish Religion, Its People, and Its History* (New York: Morrow), 168.

[87] Mark A. Noll, *Turning Points: Decisive Moments in the History of Christianity*, 2nd edition (Grand Rapids, Michigan: Baker Academic), 109.

[88] *Biblia Hebraica Stuttgartensia* (Stuttgart: German Bible Society), xi.

[89] *TANAKH: The Holy Scriptures* (New York: The Jewish Publication Society), xv.

[90] Astrid Billes Beck, "Introduction to the Leningrad Codex", *The Leningrad Codex: A Facsimile Edition* (Grand Rapids, Michigan: Eerdmans), x.

[91] Beck, xiv.

A Natural History of Scripture

[92] Victor V. Lebedev, "The Oldest Complete Codex of the Hebrew Bible", *The Leningrad Codex: A Facsimile Edition* (Grand Rapids, Michigan: Eerdmans), xxv.

[93] Kenneth Scott Latourette, *A History of Christiantiy: Volume I: to A.D. 1500*, revised edition (Peadbody, MA: Prince Press), 411.

[94] Neil Asher Silberman, *Heavenly Powers: Unraveling the Secret History of the Kabbalah* (Edison, NJ: Castle Books), 86.

[95] Noll, 183.

[96] Chidester, 302.

Chapter 8--Publishers:Elements of Microevolution

[97] John Man, *Gutenberg: How One Man Remade the World with Words* (New York: John Wiley & Sons), 103.

[98] Daneil J. Boorstin, *The Discoverers: A History of Man's Search to Know His World and Himself* (New York: Vintage Books), 510.

[99] Telushkin, 194.

A Natural History of Scripture

[100] Daniel J. Boorstin, *The Seekers: The Story of Man's Continuing Quest to Understand His World* (New York: Random House), 92.

[101] Chidester, 313.

[102] Telushkin, 205.

[103] Alister E. McGrath, *In the Beginning: the Story of the King James Bible and How It Changed a Nation, a Language, and a Culture* (New York: Doubleday), 73.

[104] Daniel J. Harrington, "Introduction to the Canon," *The New Interpreter's Bible*, vol. 1 (Nashville: Abingdon), 16.

[105] McGrath, 156.

[106] Kenneth Scott Latourette, *A History of Christianity: Volume II: A.D. 1500 to A.D. 1975*, revised edition (Peabody, MA: Prince Press), 895.

[107] Bruce L. Shelley, *Church History in Plain Language*, 2nd ed. (Nashville: Thomas Nelson), 409.

[108] Eldon Jay Epp, "Ancient Texts and Versions of the New Testament", *The New Interpreter's Bible*, vol. 8 (Nashville: Abingdon), 7.

[109] Richard Elliott Friedman, *Who Wrote the Bible?* (San Francisco: Harper), 24.

A Natural History of Scripture

[110] Karen Armstrong, *In the Beginning: A New Interpretation of Genesis* (New York: Ballantine Books), 30.

[111] Jonathan Kirsch, *Moses: A Life* (New York: Ballantine), 16.

[112] Bernard W. Anderson, *Understanding the Old Testament*, 2nd ed. (Englewood Cliffs, N.J.: Prentice-Hall), 101.

[113] Armstrong, *In the Beginning*, 10.

[114] John Barton, "Redaction Criticism", *The Anchor Bible Dictionary*, vol. 5, (New York: Doubleday), 645.

[115] Chidester, 509.

[116] Clark M. Williamson, *Has God Rejected His People?* (Nashville: Abingdon), 150.

[117] Eldon Jay Epp, "Ancient Texts and Versions of the New Testament", *The New Interpreter's Bible*, vol. 8 (Nashville: Abingdon), 3.

[118] Bart D. Ehrman, *The New Testament: A Historical Introduction to the Early Christian Writings*, 2nd ed. (New York: Oxford University Press), 443.

[119] Epp, 5.

[120] Philip W. Comfort, *EssentiaL Guide to Bible Version* (Wheaton, Illinois: Tyndale), 279-80.

A Natural History of Scripture

[121] Barbara Aland, et. al., editors, *The Greek New Testament*, 4th revised edition (Stuttgart, Germany: United Bible Societies), 3.

Conclusion

[122] Adin Steinsaltz, *The Essential Talmud* (USA: Basic Books), 272.

[123] This chart was derived from information at http://gbgm-umc.org/umw/bible/canon2.stm

[124] Fritjof Capra, *The Hidden Connections: Integrating the Biological, Cognitive, and Social Dimensions of Life into a Science of Sustainability* (New York: Doubleday), 14.

[125] See Numbers 21:14; Joshua 10:13; 1 Kings 11:41; 1 Kings 14:19; 1 Kings 14:29.

Made in the USA
Columbia, SC
31 December 2023